W9-BRJ-497

CAUSES AND CONSEQUENCES

OF THE

RISE OF JAPAN
AND THE PACIFIC RIM

CAUSES AND CONSEQUENCES

CAUSES AND CONSEQUENCES

OF THE

RISE OF JAPAN

AND THE PACIFIC RIM

STEWART ROSS

330.952

Ros

RSVP

**RAINTREE
STECK-VAUGHN**
PUBLISHERS
The Steck-Vaughn Company

Austin, Texas

© Copyright 1996, text, Steck-Vaughn Company

All rights reserved. No part of this book may be reproduced or utilized in any form or by any means, electronic or mechanical, including photocopying, recording, or by any information storage and retrieval system, without permission in writing from the Publisher. Inquiries should be addressed to:
Copyright Permissions, Steck-Vaughn Company,
P.O. Box 26015, Austin, TX 78755.

Published by Raintree Steck-Vaughn Publishers,
an imprint of Steck-Vaughn Company

Developed by the Creative Publishing Company
Editor: Sabrina Crewe
Designed by Ian Winton

Raintree Steck-Vaughn Publishers staff
Project Manager: Joyce Spicer
Editor: Shirley Shalit
Electronic Production: Scott Melcer

Cover photo (large): Downtown Tokyo at night
Cover photo (small): Hiroshima beginning to recover from the effects of the atomic bomb

Library of Congress Cataloging-in-Publication Data

Ross, Stewart.
   Rise of Japan and the Pacific Rim / Stewart Ross.
      p.   cm. – (Causes and consequences)
   Includes bibliographical references and index.
   Summary: Explains the sudden and rapid growth of the economies of Japan and the Pacific Rim countries occurring after World War II and primarily since 1960.
   ISBN 0-8172-4054-3
   1. Japan — Economic conditions — 1945- — Juvenile literature.
   2. Pacific Area — Economic conditions — Juvenile literature.
   [1. Japan — Economic conditions. 2. Pacific Area — Economic conditions.]   I. Title.   II. Series.   Rim- Eco
   HC462.9.R67   1995
   330.952'04–dc20   95-17257
                                                              CIP   AC

Printed in Hong Kong
Bound in the United States
1 2 3 4 5 6 7 8 9 0 LB 99 98 97 96 95

CONTENTS

JAPAN AND THE YOUNG TIGERS

ECONOMIC INVASION

"There is no doubt," said a businessman in a recent interview, "that the future of world business does not lie in Europe, or in the United States, or, for that matter, in Japan alone. It lies in the whole of the Pacific Rim, including the more advanced provinces of China. That's where it's at now, and that's where it will be at even more in fifty years from now."

Everyday experiences bear out the truth of this remark. Almost daily we hear of traditional Western (European or North American) industries, such as shipping and engineering, unable to match their competitors in Far Eastern countries. These countries bordering the Western Pacific, many of which have experienced very rapid economic growth since World War II, are collectively called the Pacific Rim countries. We buy a piece of electronic equipment, such as a video recorder, and the chances are that it will not have come from the United States or Britain or Germany, but from Taiwan

Hong Kong by night. The glittering array of neon signs is a vivid symbol of the region's remarkable postwar boom.

or Japan. An increasing number of cars on our roads are either made in Japan, or are Japanese models manufactured overseas. And we cannot but notice the growing range of other goods that pour into our stores and supermarkets from the factories and warehouses of the East.

OUT OF THE ASHES

In 1945 the possibility of this happening would have seemed beyond belief. Japan was in ruins. After eight years of war, the country had been pounded into an ignominious surrender by the Allies. Atomic bombs had wiped out the cities of Hiroshima and Nagasaki. Most

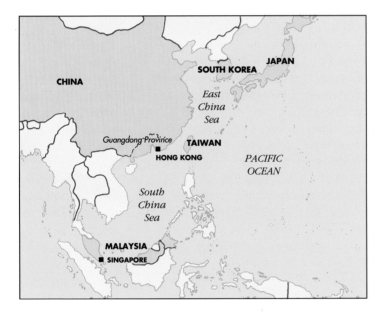

The Western Pacific Rim. Those countries focused on in this book are shaded green.

other major cities, hit by wave after wave of devastating bombing, were scarred and broken. Communications were disrupted, industry crippled, morale broken. Large numbers of foreign troops occupied mainland Japanese soil for the first time in modern history. Millions of Japanese, civilians as well as soldiers, had been killed or wounded in the fighting. Those who survived faced starvation and unemployment.

The other countries which today lead the booming Pacific Rim — Taiwan, South Korea, Singapore, Hong Kong, Malaysia, and certain regions of China — had been spared the scale of destruction which had

Gathering in the rice harvest, Taiwan, 1959. Today agriculture accounts for only a small proportion of the island's wealth.

fallen on Japan. But they were hardly better off. China, much of it economically underdeveloped and suffering from years of Japanese occupation, was slipping toward civil war between Communists and Nationalists. The island of Taiwan (then called Formosa), peopled largely by peasant farmers and fishermen, was in its industrial infancy. The British colonies of Hong Kong and Singapore, both flourishing trading bases before World War II, had suffered prolonged and crippling periods of Japanese occupation.

Korea had been in Japanese hands since 1910. Foreign settlers had encouraged agricultural and industrial development. However, with the end of the war in 1945, recent advances had been put at risk by the division of the country between the Communist north, supported by Soviet forces, and the democratic capitalist south, supported by American forces.

In 1945 Malaysia was not even a single country. Malaya and North Borneo were separate British colonies. Both had been occupied by the Japanese and both, in global terms, were economically under developed.

THE MIRACLE

So spectacular has been the advance of these nations since the grim days of 1945 that it has been popularly termed a "miracle." By 1976 Japan's GDP (gross domestic product) per head of population had overtaken Britain's, and by 1991 its total was nearly two thirds of that of the United States and still rising. Over the same period, the advance of the so-called "Young Tiger" nations of the Pacific Rim was hardly less dramatic. South Korea developed into one of the world's leading shipbuilding nations, Taiwan built up a world-class electronics industry, and Singapore and Hong Kong became important financial and manufacturing centers, boasting their own stock exchanges and banking networks. In all these countries the standard of living soared.

From 1969 to 1994 the growth rate of the Pacific Rim countries was double that of their competitors in the West. According to some estimates, by the second quarter of the twenty-first century the Chinese economy will be the biggest in the world.

In studying the extraordinary growth of these Eastern countries, this book has four aims. The first is to describe and analyze the political, social, and economic circumstances which made such growth possible. The second aim is to describe what happened and why. This will show that the region's spectacular development was, in fact, no miracle. Rather, it was achieved through a combination of factors, some of whose foundations, although not apparent, were already in place by 1945.

The book's third purpose is to detail the domestic and international consequences of the region's advance. The countries that have undergone rapid industrialization have not just grown wealthier. They have experienced urbanization on a huge scale; traditional values and family structure have come under strain. And their newfound wealth has enabled them to import Western culture, undermining still further their traditional way of life. The rise of Japan and the Pacific Rim has had a huge impact on international politics. The old Cold War division of East–West has been replaced by a three-way focus of world power: Europe (including Russia), the United States (and Latin America), and the Far East (and India), with the oil rich Arab states as an uncertain fourth dimension. Moreover, with the emergence of China as a major economic and political power, the balance is shifting further east year by year.

Finally, we conclude with a brief look into the future. Can the Western democracies hope to compete with the emerging new world order? What will be the consequences — economically, politically, militarily, and ecologically — when the full potential of China is realized? It may well be that changes already under way are forging a world entirely different from that in which we now live.

In recent years the nations of East and Southeast Asia have come to occupy an ever more important place in the world, from a strategic, political, social and economic point of view . . . [and] this has been recognized in government, business, industry and education circles alike.

From Professor Colin Mackerras, Eastern Asia: An Introductory History, 1992.

JAPAN ADVANCES

THE OPENING OF JAPAN

The sudden and rapid growth of the economies of Southeast Asia is a largely modern phenomenon, most of it occurring since 1960. Nevertheless, as Japan has been both the region's leader and example, the long-term causes of what has happened lie in the remarkable history of modern Japan.

From the 1630s onward Japan declared itself a "closed country." The Christian religion was outlawed and foreigners, especially Europeans, were shunned. Although in theory all power rested with the emperor, in practice the country was ruled by the Shogun, a powerful figure from the House of Tokugawa, assisted by a council, or Bakufu.

By the nineteenth century, contacts with Western nations began to increase. Foreign vessels called at Japanese harbors. In 1853–54 Commodore Matthew Perry of the United States Navy forced the Japanese to allow American traders into certain Japanese ports. Other nations soon followed, setting up what was known as the "treaty port" system, by which Western nations were given special rights at certain Japanese ports. Whether it liked it or not, Japan was now linked to the modern world.

Unavoidably, tensions arose between the Japanese and the foreigners, some of whom were killed. The Western nations demanded compensation, humiliating the Japanese with shows of military force. Civil discontent grew, eventually resulting in the collapse of the Shogun-Bakufu system in a coup (1868) known as the Meiji Restoration. Under the young emperor Mutsuhito, Japan began the painful path into the modern world.

THE MEIJI RESTORATION

Japan's Meiji development during the half a century before World War I (1914–18) set the course for its

future. Unlike China, which for years resolutely reject-
ed all things Western, the Japanese were prepared to
learn and adapt, to balance their old traditions with
modern ideas and inventions. They called this "cultural
borrowing." It enabled them, they realized, to be powerful enough to preserve their independence and play a
leading part in world affairs. The same ability — skill-
fully borrowing and adapting the ways of the West —
was to be an important feature of the development of
the Pacific Rim in the latter half of the twentieth century. But as Japan and other countries of Southeast
Asia were to discover, balancing the old and the new,
the traditional and the modern, was a difficult policy to
pursue. There were always those on both sides —
Westernizers and traditionalists — who believed not
enough emphasis was being given to their point of view.

Inspired by the more industrial and prosperous
nations, in 1871 the Japanese abolished the feudal
estates of the samurai (the old warrior class) and established an education system that by 1900 included 90
percent of children. Reforms to the judicial process and
the laws were started in 1871, and a Bank of Japan
was established in 1877. The emperor went to live in
the Shogun's city, which was renamed Tokyo.

Under Emperor Mutsuhito (1867–1912), Japan
developed the "emperor system" in which power formally rested with the emperor but was actually exercised by others, principally government officials. A
whole new system of government was established,
based on Western principles, with national depart-
ments, a cabinet, an advisory council, a civil service

The lower house of the Japanese par-liament in 1890. The emperor can be seen sitting on the throne behind the speaker. The chamber was modeled on the U.S. House of Representatives.

We recognize the excellence of Western civilization. We value the Western theories of rights, liberty and equality; and we respect Western philosophy and morals . . . . Above all, we esteem Western science, economics and industry. These, however, ought not to be adopted simply because they are Western; they ought to be adopted only if they can contribute to Japan's welfare.

Kuga Katsunan in the newspaper Nihon, *1889.*

A Japanese coal mine in the late nineteenth century. As in the West, coal was the prime source of energy in Japan's industrial revolution.

entered by examination, and local governments. Political parties fought for seats in a House of Representatives, elected by a very small number of people who had the right to vote. However in 1925, all men over twenty-five were given the vote. There was also a House of Peers, a mixture of hereditary and appointed dignitaries. A constitution was written in 1889.

The Japanese invited foreign experts to help with commercial, industrial, and governmental development, and Japanese students flocked to Europe and the United States. The most spectacular "raiding" of Western ideas was made by the Iwakura Mission of 1871–73. Its findings, published in five volumes in 1878, covered everything from mining to medicine.

These changes enabled Japan's economy to forge ahead. Silk production, the country's most important export, became factory-based and output rose dramatically. Factories for other products, such as glass and clothing, were opened. With the introduction of modern techniques, agricultural production tripled between 1870 and 1900. Japanese businessmen set up coal mines, steelworks, and shipbuilding yards. The country was crisscrossed with railroads and telegraph lines. By the beginning of the new century, after scarcely more than a generation of development, Japan had become a significant economic power.

Economic and industrial power inevitably offered the Japanese more political and military muscle. A modern imperial army was set up, recruited, and manned according to the 1873 Conscription Law and controlled by a new General Staff. By the end of the century, although still small, it was as well equipped and efficient as most of its Western counterparts. This was demonstrated in successful wars against China in 1894–95 and Russia in 1904–05. In 1910 Japan annexed Korea, and on the outbreak of World War I in 1914, acting with the Allies, it took the German colony of Shantung and all German Pacific islands north of the Equator.

Japan's newfound strength was soon recognized by the major powers. Agreements signed in 1894 ended the humiliating treaty ports system. Japan formed the Anglo-Japanese Alliance with Britain in 1902, and the Washington Naval Treaty with Britain and the United States in 1922. Although this limited fleets in the ratio 5–5–3 in favor of the two Western navies, and provoked outrage among the Japanese, it was an open acknowledgment that Japan was now an important force on the world scene. This had also been recognized in 1919, when Japan became a founding member of the League of Nations, along with Britain, France, and Italy.

A group of Japanese cavalry officers in 1894. By now the Japanese armed forces were already proving a major force in the Far East. Only ten years later they inflicted a series of crushing defeats on the forces of Imperial Russia.

THE CRISIS OF THE NEW JAPAN

By the mid-1920s, most of those who had come to power at the time of the Meiji Restoration had died. Japan now faced three serious problems. First was the growing power of the military and its demands for Japan to expand its influence in East Asia. Second was the inability of the elected government to control powerful groups such as the army and industrial leaders. Third were the demands of nationalists for Japan to renounce Western influence and rediscover its traditional values and customs. By 1937 these factors had undermined the small and hesitant democratic advances made over the previous seventy-five years and set Japan on a course that would bring the first phase of its modern development to a disastrous halt.

Those opposed to the new aggressive nationalism advocated liberal politics at home and a foreign policy geared to Japan's economic needs, rather than military expansion. Its foremost supporter was Shidehara Kijuro, foreign minister 1924–27 and 1929–31.

Opposition to Shidehara was voiced by various "patriotic societies" whose common aim was to "save Japan from socialism." Among the most important were Dai Nihon Kokusuikai (Japan National Essence Society, founded 1919) and Kokuhonsha (National Foundation Society, founded 1924). Membership of the latter included leading politicians, generals, and representatives from the industrial giants, the *zaibatsu*. These and other more radical groups did not advocate a particular policy. But their influence — exercised through their powerful members — gradually made moderate government impossible.

Even more dangerous in the short term were groups of army officers, such as the Cherry Society (founded 1930). They believed in the absolute supremacy of the emperor, the need for radical and decisive action to halt Japan's Westernization, and Japan's mission as guardian of Asia against the West. In practical terms they were calling for military action in China.

Following the Chinese revolution of 1911, Japan had taken advantage of that country's chaos and civil war to establish its influence north of the Great Wall. However, by 1927 the Chinese government, led by General Chiang Kai-shek, was strong enough to threaten Japan's hold. This increased the call by Japanese nationalists for military action to preserve Japan's

In every classroom is a world map or map of Asia which shows Japan in red as a very small land indeed, compared to the mainland nations of Asia . . . . In a perfectly bland manner some villager, on looking at such a map, will suggest how nice it would be to appropriate a bit more of China.

From J. F. Embree, Suye Mura: A Japanese Village, 1936.

interests in the northern Chinese province of Manchuria, rich in food, coal, and iron. Men such as the army strategist Colonel Ishiwara Kanji argued that "war can maintain war," meaning that fighting would help the Japanese economy.

Those favoring an aggressive foreign policy were helped by the harsh conditions brought about by the world economic depression that began in 1929. The value of Japanese exports fell from 2.5 billion yen a year to 1.4 billion yen a year by 1931. Rice prices fell by 50 percent and raw silk prices by almost 75 percent. The result was bankruptcy, unemployment, and unrest.

When the Tokyo government agreed to the 1930 London Naval Treaty, further limiting Japan's naval presence in the Pacific, officers in the armed forces felt humiliated. They, and many others, felt their government was weak and unpatriotic. The prime minister Hamaguchi Yuko was wounded in 1930, and his successor Inukai Tsuyoshi assassinated in 1932. These events ushered in five years of similar violent incidents. It was only a matter of time before some of the army officers decided to take matters into their own hands.

Territories occupied by the Japanese, 1931–41.

MANCHURIA AND BEYOND

On September 18, 1931, Japanese troops in Manchuria seized the city of Mukden. The soldiers acted without the consent of the government, and by the end of the year the whole of Manchuria was in Japanese hands.

Powerless to halt the action, the government was obliged to give it their support. Manchuria became the puppet state of Manchukuo, supposedly under the rule of the Chinese emperor Pu Yi, but with Japanese in all important positions. When condemned by the League

URSULINE HIGH SCHOOL LIBRARY

of Nations, Japan left the League. This put Japan outside the community of nations, with the Fascist regimes in Germany and Italy soon to follow.

The Manchurian incident heralded the downfall of party government in Japan. Amid mounting political violence, power passed to various military groupings pledged to upholding the "Japanese Way." This was marked by reverence for Emperor Hirohito (no more than a figurehead), extreme nationalism, and a belief in Japan's mission as the leader of Asia. Censorship increased. By taking the yen off the gold standard and increasing government spending, Finance Minister Takahashi Korekiyo brought Japan out of recession. Agricultural output rose and industrial output doubled between 1935 and 1939. Japan's trade with Asia increased hugely.

The most alarming part of Japan's recovery — as far as the rest of the world and Japan's long-term development were concerned — was the rapid growth in the metal, shipbuilding, and chemical industries. After 1937, much of this expansion was accounted for by military spending, which rose by 9 percent between 1933 and 1937, but by 38 percent between 1938 and 1942. This was explained by the fact that in the summer of 1937 Japan began a full-scale invasion of northern China, beginning eight disastrous years of war and bringing to a close the first phase of Japan's rise.

Japanese marines in 1932 examining the new armored car used in their attack against Shanghai.

WAR, DEFEAT, AND REBIRTH

JAPAN AT WAR

The war that had its roots in Japan's seizure of Manchuria in 1931 and brought the country into World War II at the end of 1941 marked a major interruption in Japan's rise to the status of global power. It was not, however, a complete break in that process. In this context, three points deserve attention.

First, many features of prewar Japan emerged during the period of postwar reconstruction. For example, the huge industrial combines known as *zaibatsu*, which had exercised considerable political influence during the 1930s, were supposed to have been broken up by the Americans after the war. However in the 1950s many of them reemerged in a more moderate form, but with much of their influence unchanged.

Second, policies set up as a result of the war helped the country's recovery. This included government direction of industry and trade through five-year plans. The wartime program of "industrial service to the nation" and the habit of hard work for little material reward both endured, with beneficial results, into the era of peace.

Finally, it has been argued that Japan fought not to gain an empire, but to create an environment in which the peoples of East Asia, led by Japan, would be free to develop independently. War did not achieve this aim. Nevertheless, war hastened the collapse of Western empires in Asia and prepared the ground for the spectacular economic development of Japan and its neighbors in the later twentieth century.

In 1936 the Japanese government drew up Fundamentals of National Policy, which included entering into "cordial relations" with other Asian peoples and ending the "tyrannical policies" of the Western powers in Asia. Since some politicians saw the Chinese leader Chiang Kai-shek as a tool of the United States, further conquest in China was justified as in accord with these Fundamentals. By the end of 1938

The Japanese attack on the American naval base of Pearl Harbor, Hawaii, on December 7, 1941, made war between Japan and the United States inevitable. The attack's long-term success was limited by the fact that the American carriers were not in harbor at the time.

Tianjin (formerly Tientsin), Beijing (Peking), Nanjing (Nanking), Guangzhou (Canton), and Shanghai were all in Japanese hands. The outbreak of the European war the following year further assisted the Japanese by removing Chiang's European backers from the game. The Japanese invested heavily in industrial enterprises in Manchuria, Korea, and Taiwan, a process which was to assist those countries' postwar expansion.

Some Japanese commanders had called for a full-scale war with the Soviet Union, rather than with China. However, the Japanese came off badly in border fighting with the Soviets in 1938. Despite Japan's agreements with Germany and Italy (1936 and 1940) the Soviet danger increased with the Nazi-Soviet pact of 1939. This freed the Soviet Union to turn its might on Japan if it wished, but the danger was ended by Hitler's invasion of the Soviet Union in 1941.

In 1940 Japan had introduced the concept of a Greater East Asia Co-prosperity Sphere. Had the idea been what it claimed to be (a union of states under Japanese protection for their mutual defense and economic and political welfare), then it might not have aroused the hostility it did. In fact, it was seen almost immediately as an excuse for an expansion of Japanese power in search of valuable commodities — in particular, oil, coal, rubber, iron, and other industrial metals.

This threat turned into reality in July 1941 when Japanese troops invaded Cambodia and Thailand. This move increased American anxiety over Japanese ambitions in the region. Having already frozen Japanese assets in the United States, in August 1941, President Franklin D. Roosevelt announced an oil embargo on Japan. The Dutch soon followed suit. The move confirmed Prime Minister Tojo's belief that war with the United States was likely. When further negotiations failed, on December 7, 1941, Japanese aircraft attacked the American naval base at Pearl Harbor in Hawaii.

The Allied advance into Japanese-occupied territory, 1942–45.

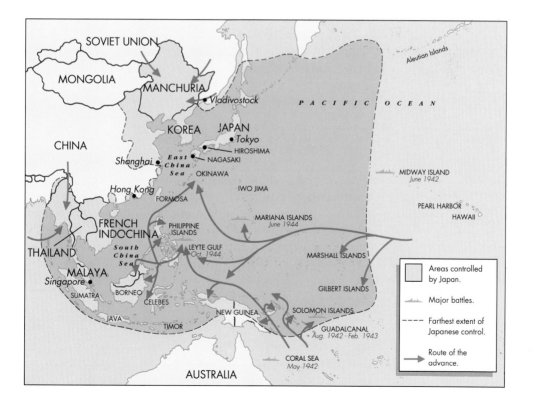

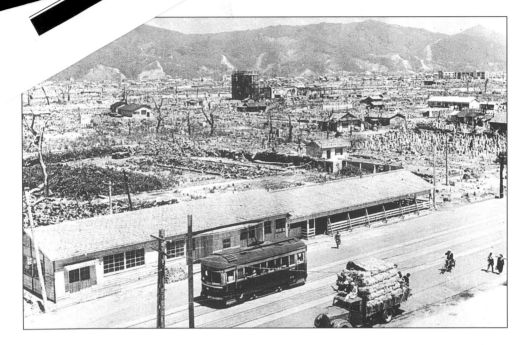

The city of Hiroshima some time after it had been the target of the first atomic bomb. Some services are running again, but an idea of the bomb's appalling destruction can be judged from the devastation in the background.

Over the next few months Japanese forces occupied a huge area of East Asia. At its widest, its territory stretched from Mongolia in the north to Timor in the south, and from Rangoon to the mid-Pacific. However, to withstand the inevitable Allied counterattack, the Greater East Asia Co-prosperity Sphere needed to become an economic reality in a very short space of time. As it was, Japanese forces of occupation were extremely brutal and unpopular, and the demands of war led to a distortion of the economies of occupied territories and a fall in living standards.

Following the naval victories of Coral Sea and Midway in 1942, the Americans and their allies used their vastly greater resources to seize all Japan's conquests. By 1945 Japan itself was being subjected to almost daily bombing on a never–before–seen scale. Finally, after the destruction of the cities of Hiroshima and Nagasaki by atomic bombs, on August 15, Emperor Hirohito authorized his country's unconditional surrender. Japan's attempt to become a world power through military force had failed.

JAPAN IN DEFEAT

At the end of the war Japan was in a dangerous condition. The people were shocked, disillusioned, humiliated, and starving. It has been estimated that, following the disbandment of the armed forces and repatriation of millions of Japanese who had been serving in occupied territories, there were as many as ten million unemployed. Following extensive war trials throughout the Far East, hundreds were executed and thousands sent to prison. Many others who had held positions in the discredited regime were banned from public life. Japan lost all the overseas possessions it had seized since the middle of the nineteenth century.

The physical destruction of the country had been enormous. The war had cost the country a quarter of its national wealth. Coal production had fallen sharply and the vital rice crop was only two-thirds of normal. Movement of goods and people was nearly impossible owing to the bombing of roads and railroads. Most industrial plants were barely operating. Life was hardest in the rubble-strewn cities, where air raids had destroyed thousands of houses and shattered the water and sewage systems. To make matters worse, all commercial activities were hampered by the hyperinflation which lasted until 1949.

The Allies, represented overwhelmingly by American troops, occupied Japan from the end of the war until a formal peace treaty with the United States came into effect in 1952. Allied control in Japan was exercised by a huge staff under General Douglas MacArthur, the Supreme Commander of the Allied Powers (SCAP). MacArthur's task was to get Japan back on its feet again, at the same time ensuring that

... the abolition of militarism and ultra-nationalism in all their forms; the disarmament and demilitarization of Japan, with continuing control over Japan's capacity to make war; the strengthening of democratic tendencies and processes in governmental, economic, and social institutions; and the encouragement and support of liberal political tendencies.

Measures to prevent Japan's reemergence as a military power, from the directive sent by Washington to General Douglas MacArthur, cited in Edward M. Martin, The Allied Occupation of Japan, *1948.*

The cost of war. In postwar Japan shortage of housing was a serious problem. A 1949 report suggested that 3.5 million new homes were needed.

General Douglas MacArthur, 1880–1964. After a brilliant career, which included distinguished service in France during World War I, MacArthur was appointed in 1941 to command the United States forces in the Far East. He accepted the Japanese surrender in 1945 and remained in Japan to oversee the country's demilitarization and reconstruction.

it would "not again become a menace to the peace and security of the world" and would develop into "a responsible and peaceful member of the family of nations." The settlement imposed by the Americans and then adapted by the Japanese themselves formed the foundation on which future recovery was built.

Under the new constitution of May 1947, sovereignty was transferred from the emperor to the people and Japan became a demilitarized state. The emperor was retained as a figurehead, but the House of Peers was abolished along with the peerage system. A House of Councillors and House of Representatives made up a new elected diet, with the prime minister and cabinet chosen from among the representatives. After a certain amount of political chaos, the system settled down to provide a series of conservative governments dominated, after 1955, by the Liberal Democrat Party.

One cause of Japan's conservatism was the land reform imposed by SCAP. This broke up large estates by forcing absentee landlords to sell their surplus land, thereby creating a country of prosperous, conservative small farm owners. Attempts to destroy the *zaibatsu* were less successful, and ten years after the war Mitsubishi and other larger concerns were back in full-scale operation. Similarly, the dismissal of those who had worked for the military government was being reconsidered by 1949, allowing back into positions of authority men of experience and conservative outlook.

All these measures helped create the stable atmosphere in which Japan's economy could begin to recover. Another factor was the provision by the state of nine years of compulsory, free education for all children. This was important not just because it sought to raise future generations in the ways of "truth and justice," but also because it provided Japan with a skilled workforce.

THE ROAD BACK

The recovery of the Japanese economy started slowly. Then, based on the security provided by SCAP's military presence and the sound constitutional settlement, it rapidly gathered pace. By 1955 Japan's growth was faster than that of any other industrialized nation. Taking Japan's industrial output in 1934–35 as 100, in 1948 it had fallen to 55. Within two years it had risen to 84, and within another five years to an amazing 181. How had this happened?

Some of the reasons for Japan's remarkable recovery have already been mentioned. They include the creation of a relatively stable, business-oriented political system, mass education, and the emergence of a large, prosperous class of small farm owners which provided a ready market for industry's goods. Also important was Article IX of the new constitution, known as the peace clause. This declared that "The Japanese people forever renounce war as a sovereign right of the nation." Because of this declaration and strict limits imposed on the country's armed forces, at a time when most other nations were engaged in crippling military spending, the Japanese were able to concentrate on investment and output that had a purely commercial purpose.

Surprisingly, some effects of the war helped Japan's recovery once the fighting was over. People had become used to working long hours for low pay. This helped keep down the price of Japanese goods and so made them more attractive in world markets. The government's experience of directing the economy stood it in good stead when it came to managing the recovery.

Finance Minister Ishibashi Tanzan established an Economic Stabilization Board to coordinate production. The five-year plan of 1948, designed to lift production levels to those of 1938, used experience gained

Millions might have perished if it had not been for the speedy relief given by the United States Army [in 1945]. Similarly, our industry was completely at a standstill for lack of materials . . . . It was only with the assistance of the United States that it was revived and restored. For all these, our people will remain ever grateful.

At the same time . . . we admit that there was another aspect of the Occupation which is less commendable . . . . A purge was enforced which deprived our nation of a trained body of men at a crucial moment: the financial concerns were disintegrated by a complete break up of Zaibatsu . . . notorious Communist leaders were released from prison . . . education was reformed, sapping the moral fibre of our bewildered youth . . . .

From Yoshida Shigeru (prime minister of Japan 1946 and 1948–54), The Yoshida Memoirs, 1961.

Clock manufacture in a converted arms factory, 1945. Almost all the clocks were for export, as they were too expensive for most Japanese.

from the wartime five-year plan. A Reconstruction Bank (later renamed the Development Bank) directed capital to vital areas, such as food, iron, steel, and coal production. Because most of its production plants had been destroyed, Japanese industry reequipped with the latest technology. The demands of war had also stimulated technological progress in areas such as electronics, shipbuilding, and engineering. Finally, there was the question of pride. Once the shock of defeat and occupation had worn off, the Japanese were determined to reestablish their sense of national pride and identity by proving that, although they had not been able to defeat the West in battle, they could prove its equal in the marketplace.

Also crucial in Japan's recovery was the help given by the United States. This extended far beyond the initial work of SCAP in getting the country moving again and providing it with a constitutional framework. By 1948 the United States was beginning to see Japan as a potential ally rather than a defeated enemy. The cause of this change was the intensification of the Cold War between the United States and the Soviet Union. Japan became an even more important factor in United States foreign policy the following year, when China fell to the Communist forces of Mao Zedong.

The United States was determined that Japan should not fall into the Communist sphere of influence. When the purge of former wartime officials was being reconsidered, a new purge — this time of left-wing sympathizers — took place. In the Red Purge of 1949,

22,000 men with socialist or Communist sympathies were removed from office. The Americans also assisted the regrowth of Japanese industry with business experience, investment, and technology. Even more helpful was American spending in Japan during the Korean War of 1950–53. In 1951 American spending in Japan amounted to $600 million, rising to $800 million over the next two years. When the war was over, the United States poured aid into countries formerly occupied by the Japanese. The grants — $200 million to Burma (Myanmar) and $550 million to the Philippines, for example — were earmarked for spending on Japanese exports. This money was vitally important in helping Japan expand her export markets.

The U.S.–Japanese link was formalized with the 1954 Mutual Security Agreement, which brought further American spending into Japan. Some Japanese resented such close dependence on the United States, which they saw as merely a new form of Western imperialism. The Americans, they claimed, were more interested in Japanese stability than in whether the country was a true democracy. Supporters of the policy argued, with some justification, that temporary partnership with the United States enabled Japan to build up its strength. And that, they concluded, was the only path to true independence and influence.

The miracle begins — high quality, low cost Japanese trucks pouring off the assembly line, 1949.

THE JAPANESE MIRACLE

THE WORLD'S NEW WORKSHOP

Average annual growth rates of the world's major economies, 1870–1992. Since 1913 (excluding the war years) Japan has out-stripped all competitors.

The spectacular and sustained growth of the Japanese economy was one of the most remarkable features of the postwar world. Two fifths the size of Britain's economy in 1955, by 1992 the Japanese economy was triple that of Britain. By 1980 it was turning out more steel and cars than the United States. In the 1990s the Japanese economy — the second largest in the world and the leader in many important fields — was 15 percent of the world total.

Japan's postwar growth advanced in four phases. First came the immediate recovery during the period of

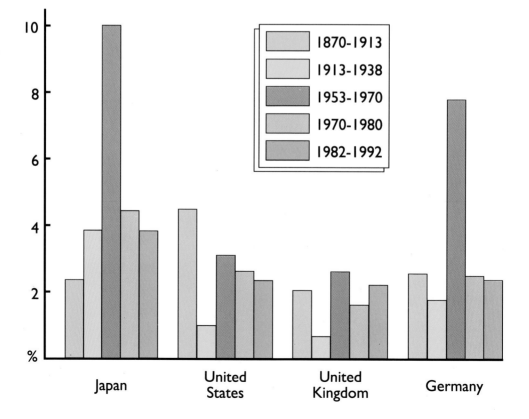

Legend:
- 1870-1913
- 1913-1938
- 1953-1970
- 1970-1980
- 1982-1992

Japan · United States · United Kingdom · Germany

By the 1980s Japan was one of the leaders in the global communications revolution. Here work is taking place on a satellite to keep watch over the world's oceans.

American occupation, dealt with in the previous chapter. This was followed by a rapid increase up to the oil crisis of 1973. Over the next eight years the rate of Japan's economic growth slowed, before picking up again in the 1980s.

As we have seen, taking 1934–35 levels as 100, by 1955 Japanese output had reached 181. By 1960 it had reached 410 and continued to grow at a rate of 13.2 percent per year until the early 1970s. It was led by conglomerates, known as *keiretsu*, not unlike the old *zaibatsu*, which managed many small firms under an umbrella, or protective, organization. These conglomerates had fixed production quotas and shared raw materials. The largest of these conglomerates, such as Mitsubishi, Mitsui, Sumitomo, and Fuji, contained more than seventy smaller firms. The emphasis was on industries requiring high technology, a high level of investment, and large-scale use of imported raw materials, such as iron ore and oil. For example, Japanese oil imports rose from 207 million barrels in 1960 to 1.3 billion barrels ten years later.

Japanese industrialists were among the first to develop the use of robots as a way of combating mounting labor costs. This "Spider Robot" was built in 1994 to climb gas storage tanks and search for faults.

During the 1960s industrial output rose by 373 percent. Steel production increased from 22 to 93 million tons. A high proportion of this was used in Japan's flourishing shipbuilding industry, which launched 1.76 million tons of shipping in 1960 and 12.65 million tons in 1970. Over the same period of time production of Japanese passenger cars rose from a meager 165,000 to over 3 million, and television sets from 3.6 million to 13.8 million.

Although it had a large and thriving home market, Japan came increasingly to depend on exports. Its largest trading partner was the United States, with whom it conducted about 30 percent of its trade. Australia provided much of its iron ore, and the Middle East a growing proportion of its oil. For the first time since the war, in 1965 Japanese exports were more valuable than its imports. This trend increased into the 1990s. By 1978 Japan had a trade surplus (the difference in value between imports and exports) of $24 billion. By 1987 this had risen to $190 billion. By the 1980s it was accompanied by huge Japanese investment overseas. By 1992, 600 factories in the United States were Japanese-owned. In anticipation of the 1992 single European market, investment in Europe, particularly Britain, also rose sharply.

In the early stages of recovery the strongest selling point of Japanese goods was their low price. This was possible because of the comparatively low cost of labor. By the 1960s, however, Japan's wages were no longer among the lowest in the world. In response, although price remained a key factor in selling, Japanese manufacturers changed their strategy. "Made in Japan" became a byword for quality, reliability, and after-sales service. This was particularly so in the electronics and automobile industries. The East Europeans and even the Italians might produce cheaper cars, but no one could compete with the Japanese for a combination of price and quality. Similarly, electrical goods manufactured in Taiwan and Hong Kong were cheaper than their Japanese counterparts, but products bearing such names as Sony, JVC, and Hitachi had a reputation for being among the best money could buy.

When the Arab-Israeli War of 1973 led to a massive rise in world oil prices, the period of Japan's phenomenal growth came to an abrupt halt. In 1974 the wholesale price index rose by 31 percent and the rise in Japan's gross national product (GNP) slowed for the first time since the war. The second oil price rise of 1979–80 caused another dip. However, showing remarkable flexibility and good business sense, the country weathered the storm and entered upon what has been termed the "second economic miracle." Although in the 1980s the growth in real incomes did not match the 10 percent annual growth of the 1960s, at 5 percent it was still way ahead of most industrial nations.

The new growth was achieved by cutting the country's dependence upon oil and switching industrial output away from production that required massive energy consumption and expensive imports of raw materials. The amount of electricity generated by oil-fired stations fell by almost half in ten years, and by 1985 one quarter of Japan's electricity was coming from nuclear power. Industrial production shifted from large-scale engineering to high-value, high-technology manufacture, such as computers, semiconductors, and microprocessors. By the mid-1980s, 60 percent of the world's robots were in Japanese factories. As a result of this change, despite the enormous advances made by other Pacific Rim countries in the final quarter of the twentieth century, Japan's economy in 1994 accounted for three quarters of that of the entire region.

WHY JAPAN?

It is much easier to describe Japan's success in the second half of the twentieth century than to explain why it happened. How much, for example, was due to the help given to Japan by the Americans during the period of the Occupation? Equally controversial is the role of the Japanese government. For example, did the government provide the right background for the economy to flourish, or was its role more active? There are no simple answers to these questions. Nevertheless, there are four major factors that help explain why Japan earned an increasing share in the overall expansion of world wealth since World War II.

The first and most obvious is the work undertaken during the Occupation, both in settling the country down and giving it a base from which the recovery could begin. Four points need to be emphasized — the stability provided by the new constitution, the creation of a large, prosperous class of small farmers, the provision for universal education (with 30 percent of the population going on to post-high school education) and the massive spending in Japan by the United States as a result of the Cold War and the Korean War.

The second factor, Japan's political stability, grows out of the first. But even this is controversial — to what extent was stability a cause of prosperity, or a consequence of it? There can be no definitive answer to this. All we can say is that with business backing, the Democratic and Liberal parties combined in 1955 to form the Liberal Democrat Party. The new party held power continually until 1993, providing a stable, business-oriented administration.

The sustained success of the Liberal Democrats was explained by the support of the farmers' vote, its ample funds, its clever use of influence, and the lack of organized opposition. More important were its close links with government and business. The prewar practice of appointing ex-civil servants to government office was continued. Prime Minister Yoshida, for example, had been a diplomat before 1941. In the twenty-five years from 1955 to 1980 ex-government officials held the office of prime minister for all but five years. The government's links with business were made not through individual corporations, as they were before the war, but with umbrella organizations, such as the Japan Chamber of Employers' Organizations, the

I do not see them [the Japanese] becoming a fractious, contentious society like America, always debating and knocking each other down. That is not in their culture. They want growth and they want to get on with life. They are not interested in ideology as such, or in the theory of good government. They just know a good government and want a good government.

Lee Kuan Yew (prime minister of Singapore 1959–90) on the 1993 change of government in Japan, cited in The Economist, *1993.*

Japan Chamber of Commerce and Industry, and the Federation of Economic Organizations.

The Liberal Democrats' backing of industrial and commercial enterprise, growing out of their close partnership with business, was the third factor in Japan's development. The Ministry of International Trade and Industry (MITI) played a crucial role. One of its most important measures was to encourage the formation of *keiretsu*, and MITI sponsored a change in the antimonopoly laws to allow their formation. It also spurred on the shift from heavy industry to "knowledge-intensive" industries from the mid-1970s onward, sponsoring the famous Fifth Generation Computer project in 1981.

The government also helped business expansion by working with the Economic Planning Agency to establish the country's five- and ten-year economic plans. It was also responsible for reforming the taxation system (to encourage investment), keeping inflation low, using foreign exchange controls to divert raw materials to individual companies, and arranging cooperation agreements with other countries to give the Japanese access to the latest technology at favorable prices.

Heavy government expenditure in infrastructure, especially roads and railroads, improved communications and business efficiency and gave work to Japanese firms. In 1960 Japan had only 162,000

Healthy working practices — employees at a shipyard perform a daily exercise routine. Japanese companies take greater responsibility for workers' health and recreation than their Western counterparts.

miles of paved road. By 1975 the figure had risen to 207,600 miles. In the 1970s, as a result of such expenditure, Japan had the highest level of public debt in the industrialized world. Unlike many Western countries, however, government spending went on projects of long-term commercial value, not social services. In 1984–86, for example, Japanese spending on social security was half that of West Germany. As a proportion of GNP, the figure was even lower.

The final factor in Japan's growth lay in the attitudes and performance of individual workers, companies, and *keiretsu*. Western thinkers and industrialists found these the most difficult aspect of Japan's development to get to grips with. For example, the excellent relations between workforce and management, which led to high productivity and a very low number of days being lost through strikes, were rooted in Japan's history (although, when they did occur in the 1950s, strikes were ruthlessly crushed). Some experts say the origins of this good relationship lay not in business practice but in a culture and religion that emphasized responsibility and loyalty.

Features worthy of note include the practice of workers remaining with the same company all their working lives, and the company taking greater responsibility for them than was customary in the West. This took the form of investment in training, health care, and recreation. The social division between worker and management, such a prominent feature in much of the West, was far less prominent in Japan.

Until the 1960s the Japanese economy was helped by low wage rates. What surprised most economists was that when wages rose, they did so slower than productivity yet faster than in competitor countries. The average Japanese household saved far more than the average household in the West — in 1970–72 it amounted to 26 percent of disposable income, compared with 16 percent in the West. Through investment, these savings were available for loan to business and commerce. Another feature of Japanese business practice was rising investment in research and development. In 1967 it was 1.7 percent of national income. By 1988 it had grown to 3.3 percent, higher than that in West Germany and equal to that of the United States. Expenditure on research and development enabled Japanese industry to increase productivity ahead of its rivals and give the country a technological lead that was the envy of the rest of the industrialized world.

THE NEW JAPAN

THE ENVIRONMENT

Anyone visiting Japan today, particularly the Pacific Coast on the main island of Honshu, is immediately struck by the immensity of the urban sprawl. This brings home two of the more pronounced consequences of Japan's postwar development — population rise and urbanization.

In 1950 the population of Japan was about 83 million. By the mid-1980s it had climbed to some 120 million. This increase was not caused by a rise in the birthrate, which fell from 34.9 births per thousand of population in 1920, to 18.2 in 1955 and 11.9 in 1985. The declining birthrate was accounted for by the practice of birth control and by women marrying on an average of two years later than they had done in the middle of the century.

The reason for the rise in population was a dramatic improvement in the health of the population. Prosperity enabled the Japanese to become fitter, stronger, larger (the average boy was almost eight inches taller in 1976 than in 1950), and to live longer.

All aboard! Japanese commuters are prepared to put up with conditions on overcrowded trains that would evoke howls of protest in the West.

By the mid-1980s the expectation of life was the highest in the world — seventy-four years for men and over eighty years for women.

It was estimated that by the year 2000 15 percent of the Japanese population would be over sixty-five. The aging of the population produced the same fear as in other prosperous nations — that the number of retired elderly people would put a huge strain on an economy sustained by an ever-decreasing workforce. By 1986 Japan was already spending 5 percent of its GNP on health care. However, unlike the situation in some Western nations such as Britain, the bulk of the funding was undertaken by private insurance, not the government.

Urbanization accompanied and even outstripped the rise in population. Immediately after World War II, about half of the nation's workforce was composed of small farmers. By 1980 less than 14 percent of the workforce was engaged in agriculture, forestry, or fishing; and agriculture accounted for only 2.5 percent of GNP. In 1960, 64 percent of the population lived in towns and cities, a quarter in the largest 21 cities. By 1975 the proportion had risen to over 75 percent and was still rising. This led various governments to devise ways of encouraging the government offices and businesses to move away from the overcrowded and heavily polluted urban centers. By the early 1990s, none of the plans had proved very successful.

Between 1950 and the mid-1980s the Japanese population increased by almost 50 percent. The average number of people occupying each square mile of Japan in 1991 compares dramatically with other nations, as this graph shows.

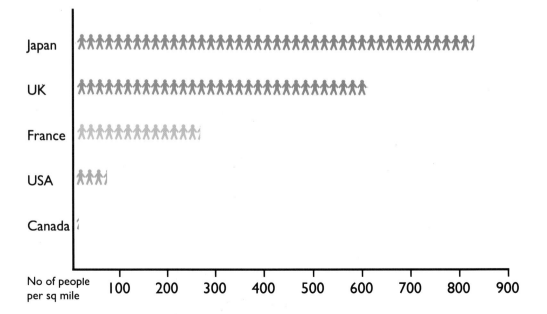

| No of people per sq mile | 100 | 200 | 300 | 400 | 500 | 600 | 700 | 800 | 900 |

Shoppers in Tokyo revive themselves at the oxygen bar in a department store.

Pollution was first recognized as a major scandal in the 1960s. The close partnership between commerce and government ensured that until then environmental issues were less important than increased output. The result was a horrific despoilation of the land, sea, and air. Coastal waters were poisoned by sewage and industrial waste material, killing fish stocks. The atmosphere in the large cities became smog-laden and almost unbreathable, to the extent that Tokyo traffic police were issued oxygen. Asthma cases increased dramatically. Rivers were killed and even the earth was poisoned by toxic waste. The greatest scandal concerned the wholesale mercury poisoning of the town of Minamata, which killed sixty people and injured hundreds.

Faced with a growing public outcry, the government acted in 1966 to regulate car exhaust emissions. A comprehensive Pollution Prevention Law followed the next year, enforced after 1971 by an Environmental Agency. By the 1990s, although pollution was still a major problem, the situation was at least more carefully monitored and controlled.

SOCIETY

The traditional Japanese family had been made up of several generations living in the same household. Industrialization changed this, the average size of the Japanese family falling from 4.97 in 1955 to 3.17 thirty years later. The pressure on parents to pay for their children's education through high school to university was another reason for the fall in the birthrate — only the very wealthy could afford to educate more than two children. By the later 1980s the typical Japanese family consisted of a father, who spent long hours out of the home at work, a mother in control of all domestic matters, including the budget and the education and welfare of the children, and one or two offspring. There was a tendency for more women to undertake part-time work, but only during the hours that the children were at school. The Western customs of child-minding and baby-sitting were not well regarded in Japan.

Although women had the same legal rights as men, even in the 1980s it was not easy for a single woman to pursue her career at a high level. Secretarial jobs were plentiful but, compared with Western nations, there were very few women in the top positions. Both men and women were expected to marry, but the incidence of arranged marriages — O miai — had fallen to 25 percent by 1986.

The abolition of the peerage, the loss of personal wealth owing to the war, and the redistribution of land during the Occupation meant that education became a vital ladder to a successful career. The proportion of the population remaining in education past the minimum school leaving age rose from 43 percent in 1950 to 94 percent in 1980.

Pressure for places at the best schools and universities was fiercely competitive. The best jobs did not depend so much on an individual's level of education, but on the institution they had attended. High academic demands were made on even the youngest children. A survey conducted among Tokyo's elementary schoolchildren in 1988 found that three-quarters of them attended extra lessons during the summer vacation. Twenty-five percent of them had no vacation!

By the end of the 1980s Japan had some two million university students in about five hundred universities. Again, the competition to get into the better ones, such as the University of Tokyo and Keio University, was ferocious. Mental breakdowns and even suicide among students were the inevitable results of such pressure.

Hard work brought the Japanese immense material benefits. Moreover, partly as a result of the pressure applied by large trade unions, wealth was more evenly distributed than in many Western countries. It is interesting that student protests of the late 1960s were less concerned with attacking the rich than with opposing the pursuit of wealth.

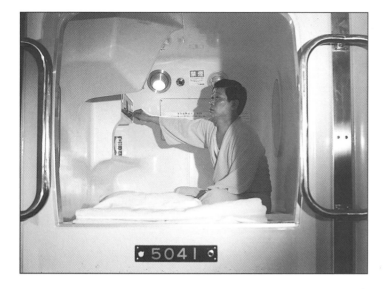

A hotel "room" in Osaka — the population density in Japan has caused such a severe shortage of space that capsule hotels are often the only option for people seeking a place to stay.

Incomes soared to some of the highest levels in the world. Eating patterns changed and Japanese homes boasted the full range of modern electronic gadgetry — television, video recorders, microwaves, and computers. By 1990 there was an average of almost two color televisions in every household, and homes without telephones and refrigerators were almost unknown. Pollution, urban density, and an efficient public transportation network kept the level of car ownership below that of the United States and Germany.

There were areas, however, in which Japan still lagged behind other industrial nations. Two of the most significant were hours of work and housing. While a forty-hour week was coming to be seen as unusually long in the West, in Japan fifty hours was not uncommon. A serious shortage of land kept the price of houses and apartments worryingly high. By the 1980s the Japanese were taking out mortgages over two generations to buy their homes. And the quality of housing was below Western standards, too. Millions of people had to put up with tiny, cramped apartments. In 1980 only one third of Japanese dwellings were connected to a main sewage system.

POLITICS AND CULTURE

The close partnership between the Liberal Democrat government and the business community had further consequences during the period of Japan's so-called "economic miracle." One was widespread student

The younger generation of Japanese have welcomed most aspects of Western culture, including its trendy "junk food" outlets.

The march of Japanese cultural disintegration appears to be slow but insidious.

Iwao Minami, cited in Peter Berger and Hsin-Huang Hsiao, In Search of an East Asian Development Pattern, *1988.*

unrest, particularly during the 1960s. At its height, in October 1969, there were disputes raging in no less than 77 universities.

The unrest was worldwide, and its causes were complex. In Japan it arose out of the younger generation's disillusionment with years of conservative rule. In particular, it was a rebellion against the environmental effects of pollution, political corruption, the lack of governmental concern for social welfare, and the unchecked drive for wealth. The most telling slogan was the cry "Kutabareta GNP!" — "Down with GNP!" In the end the movement faded away because it lacked an organized program, although Marxist terrorist bands survived into the 1970s.

Some historians of Japanese politics argued that the students' complaints were not without foundation. They claimed that postwar Japan was not a true democracy. Power did not rest with the people, they said, but with interest groups that controlled the government. Some support for this view came when, from time to time, serious financial scandals were uncovered. Prime Minister Tanaka Kakuei resigned as a result of a bribery scandal in 1974, and a scandal involving illegal political donations and stock trading-brought down the Takeshita government in 1989.

Was Japan a Western or Asian country? This question concerned the Japanese ever since they decided to become an industrial and technological power. In many ways late twentieth century Japan was a Western country. Its new architecture, transportation systems, and business patterns were just like those of Europe and the United States, and so were its systems of government, education, administration, and trade unions. In music, literature, and the arts Japanese tastes were very much like those of its main business competitors. Surveys showed, too, that attitudes to work, religion, and morality were Western.

By the 1980s, however, the Japanese were beginning to feel that, in adopting the ways of the West, they were losing touch with their roots. This feeling was strengthened when some of their Pacific Rim competitors, such as Singapore and China, appeared to be successfully developing a culture that balanced Western ideas with traditional Asian ones. As a result, some Japanese made a conscious effort to rediscover their past. From 1975 onward, for example, Japanese prime ministers made controversial visits to the Yasukuni Shrine, honoring the country's executed war criminals as well as victims of the war. In addition to this, the public sorrow at the death of Emperor Hirohito in 1989 was widespread and genuine throughout the country. The "economic miracle" had both lifted Japan's self-confidence and enabled it once more to be proud of its national heritage.

The funeral of Emperor Hirohito, February 24, 1989. To the surprise of some observers, who believed the emperor had become little more than a figurehead, Hirohito's death evoked widespread public mourning.

INTO THE FAMILY OF NATIONS

JAPAN AND THE WORLD IN 1945

This American poster (1944) was typical of the Allies' anti-Japanese wartime propaganda. Suspicion of the Japanese remained long after the war had ended.

A t the end of World War II Japan stood lower in the eyes of the world than at any other time in its history. Whether they deserved it or not, the Japanese were regarded as an unbelievably cruel and tyrannical people who had sought to conquer a massive Asian empire through military force. In particular, their harsh treatment of conquered peoples and of prisoners of war was universally despised. Even the action of the young Japanese suicide pilots — the *kamikaze* — was seen as dangerous fanaticism rather than desperate bravery. The horrible suffering of the Japanese civilian population, culminating in the destruction of Hiroshima and Nagasaki by atomic bombs, was somehow regarded as just punishment for a wicked people.

Long after German war crimes had been accepted as the work of an evil minority, no such understanding was extended to the Japanese. The view of the Japanese as cruel warmongers was perpetuated in countless novels and films. It seemed that the world would never forget the war in Asia, and certainly never forgive the Japanese for their part in it. A 1992 survey illustrated Japan's problem. It found that 29 percent of Indonesians, 37 percent of

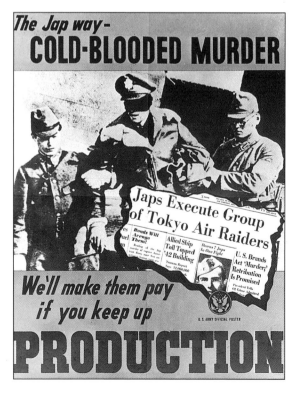

The Jap way —
COLD-BLOODED MURDER

Japs Execute Group of Tokyo Air Raiders

We'll make them pay if you keep up

PRODUCTION

Filipinos, and 40 percent of Malaysians felt they could never forget the bad aspects of Japan's behavior in World War II.

This situation had an immense impact on postwar Japan, promoting a burning desire to live down the past. In domestic matters, as we have seen, it fed a determined effort to rebuild national pride by economic rather than military success. In foreign affairs it promoted an inward-looking policy of pacifism and noninvolvement.

ALLIES ACROSS THE PACIFIC

For the first thirty years of the postwar period Japan's foreign policy rested on three key principles. The first and most important was alliance with the United States. This began with the Japan-United States Security Treaty of 1951, renewed in 1960 and every ten years thereafter. The alliance brought Japan several advantages. It ensured an open market in the United States for Japanese goods, enabled the government to concentrate on economic development by not having to spend large sums on defense, and ensured protection against possible threat from its Communist neighbors, the Soviet Union and China.

Even so, the policy of being a "free rider" beneath the United States defense umbrella had its disadvantages. For example, the Japanese government was drawn into unpopular support for the American forces in the Vietnam War and, by recognizing the Nationalist government in Taiwan, Japan was prevented from taking advantage of the gigantic Chinese market until the early 1970s. The alliance also drew much hostility at home. Of the five Japanese prime ministers in office from 1954 to 1972, three fell from power because of foreign affairs. Before the renewal of the Security Treaty in 1960, there were violent anti-American demonstrations, leading to a cancellation of a proposed visit by President Dwight Eisenhower.

The second principle of Japanese foreign policy — keeping defense spending to a minimum — was closely related to the United States alliance. During the Occupation Japan was permitted to establish a small Self Defense Force, which numbered 165,000 by 1954. Following gradual withdrawal of American forces, it grew to 235,000 by 1972 and included tanks, missiles, 900 airplanes, and 200 small ships. Even so, defense

Land, sea and air forces will never be maintained. The Japanese people forever renounce war as a sovereign right of the nation, and the threat or use of force as a means of settling international disputes.

Article IX of the Japanese Constitution.

The successful 1964 Tokyo Olympics were a clear sign that Japan had been readmitted to the world community.

spending (except in the early years) stayed to within one percent of GNP, and Japan stuck to the three non-nuclear principles of Prime Minister Sato Eisaku: Japan would neither manufacture nuclear weapons nor possess them or permit their installation on Japanese soil. While massive defense spending crippled economies such as that of the Soviet Union, Japanese finance ministers were able to gear their policies to expanding trade and productive manufacture, raising the GNP from $24.6 billion in 1955 to $2.8 trillion in 1989.

This tied in with the third foreign policy principle — directing diplomacy to commercial rather than political ends, concentrating largely on the countries of the Pacific Basin (the Pacific islands and the countries bordering the Pacific). More than 70 percent of Japan's trade was directed toward this region. Even the Middle East, from where Japan drew most of its oil supplies, attracted little diplomatic attention until the oil crisis of 1973.

Guided by these three principles, Japanese foreign policy was a notable success. It helped dispel the country's warlike image and gain it admission into the community of nations. Japan was admitted to the United Nations in 1956 and later joined the General Agreement on Tariffs and Trade (GATT) and the Organization for Economic Co-operation and Development (OECD). The holding of the Olympic Games in Tokyo in 1964 was a concrete symbol of the world's acceptance of the new Japan.

However, by the 1970s the situation was beginning to change. As one of the world's most powerful economies, Japan had to accept that power carried responsibilities. In the economic sphere, for example, many countries looked to Japan for a lead. As a result, by the 1990s Japan was no longer a spectator of world politics, but a key participant.

JAPAN IN THE MODERN WORLD

As we have seen, many Japanese — particularly those on the political left — had never been happy with their country's close military alliance with the United States. By the 1970s Japan's position was coming under criticism from within the United States as well. Tension between the two countries arose on two counts. The first was a feeling in the United States that Japan should bear more responsibility for its own defense. The second was American complaints at the growing imbalance of trade between the two countries.

Under pressure from the United States, in 1961 and 1970 Japan agreed to build up her Defense Force to take some of the strain off the American defense budget. As this immediately raised the fear of reemergent Japanese imperialism among its Asian neighbors, the change was made only gradually. Nevertheless, in the 1980s Japan dropped its ceiling on defense expenditure and by the 1990s its defense budget was among the largest in the world.

Because of its total reliance on importing raw materials, however, great care was taken to emphasize the defensive capacity of the Japanese military. Its stated aim was to be able to defend Japanese shores and all sea-lanes to a distance of one thousand miles from Japanese ports, thereby safeguarding the passage of goods. One of the first signs of Japan's newfound independence from the United States came in 1979, when it ignored American pressure and continued to take oil imports from Iran when the American

The combined military budgets of Japan . . . [and her major East-Asian trading partners, including China] are about 6 per cent of world military expenditures, with Germany alone at 5 per cent and the United States at 30 per cent. Although there may be some argument about the exact numbers, Asia's do seem to be small. Japan accounts for half the military budget of the area and does not seem bent on combat.

From James C. Abegglen, Sea Change: Pacific Asia as the New World Industrial Center, *1994.*

Japan's Self Defense Force on parade. There has been mounting pressure for this well-equipped and efficient fighting force to play a greater part in peacekeeping outside of East Asia.

Embassy there was under siege. The most serious challenge to the U.S.–Japan alliance came in 1990–91. In response to Iraq's invasion of Kuwait, the United States led a multinational United Nations force against Iraq. Japan's contribution — minesweepers and $9 billion — was felt to be inadequate from one of the United States' closest allies.

In 1958 Japan's imports from the United States were worth $980 million, while its exports to the United States amounted to only $666 million. Fifteen years later the situation had been reversed, imports valuing $8.3 billion and exports $9.6 billion. The Americans, and other countries trading with Japan, complained that this favorable balance of trade was achieved by unfair practices that hampered the export of manufactured goods to Japan. In 1971 the United States had imposed a damaging surcharge, or additional tax, on Japanese imports.

In 1973 the Japanese government responded by making it easier for foreign imports to enter Japan. Nevertheless, the difficulty of selling to Japanese markets persisted. At one time or another during the 1970s and 1980s there were complaints about unfair practice regarding the markets in steel, cars, fruit and other agricultural products, semi-conductors, and building contracts. European manufacturers joined their counterparts in the United States to condemn Japanese protectionism. On each occasion Japan reacted cautiously, gradually opening its domestic markets to foreign trade. Despite these measures, the feeling persisted into the 1990s that Japan was not doing enough to assist world trade.

Japan responded to such criticism in two ways. It blamed the United States for its own economic problems, saying that successive governments had failed to keep military spending in line with the country's wealth. The second response was to do more to share its wealth with the rest of the world. In 1977 it agreed to keep annual economic growth at 7 percent, a figure it failed to maintain. As the country with the world's largest trade surplus ($95 billion in 1988), Japan stepped up overseas aid to over $8 billion by the end of the decade. At the same time Japan's contributions to United Nations peacekeeping forces rose to third place behind the United States and the Soviet Union. Japanese money and, sometimes, personnel were used in trouble spots as far apart as Nicaragua and Afghanistan. Japan also increased its contributions to

Finally, the international community expects greater sharing of Japan's economic wealth. The internationalization of Japan must proceed both internally and externally. Japan must expand the international community's access to its domestic workings and it must share more of its wealth and experience with the world. Japan indeed faces daunting post-Cold War challenges as well as expanded opportunities to contribute to the construction of a new world order.

From Tsuneo Akaha, Japan's Post-Cold War Challenges and Opportunities in Asia Pacific, 1992.

United Nations relief agencies. The country's greater commitment to world peace and prosperity was set out in 1988 by Prime Minister Takeshita Noboru's International Co-operation Initiative.

In line with its more important role in world affairs, Japan's foreign policy became more political. It joined the Arab boycott of Israel and gave aid to countries such as Pakistan and Egypt because of their strategic importance. Eager to bring peace to the Pacific Rim, Japanese diplomats helped mediate in war-torn Cambodia.

Finally, and perhaps most significantly of all, from the 1970s onward Japan deliberately supported the economies of the Pacific Rim. The aim was to build up the region into a huge trading area, based around Japanese manufacture and raw materials from countries such as China (coal), Indonesia (oil), and Australia (iron and bauxite). More than any other nation, Japan was responsible for the rapid economic development of South Korea, eastern China, Taiwan, Hong Kong, Singapore, and Malaysia. To counteract worries that it was trying to recreate the Co-prosperity Sphere, Japan provided massive loans, particularly to China and South Korea. It also changed the emphasis from the Pacific Rim to the Pacific Basin, thereby including the United States and Canada in its plan.

Leaders of the Asia-Pacific Economic Co-operation group at a world trade conference in Seattle in 1993. From left to right: New Zealand prime minister James Bolger, Indonesian president Suharto, Singapore prime minister Goh Chok Tong, Philippines president Fidel Ramos, U.S. president Bill Clinton, Taiwan representative Vincent Siew, Japanese prime minister Morihiro Hosokawa, and Hong Kong financial secretary Hamish MacLeod.

THE RISE OF THE YOUNG TIGERS

DEFINITIONS

The average annual growth rate of GDP (gross domestic product) in Pacific Rim countries, 1988–92. The United States figure for the same period was only 1.6 percent.

Economists divide the economically significant Pacific nations into six groupings: (1) the United States and Canada; (2) Japan; (3) China; (4) the Asian NICs (Newly Industrializing Countries) — South Korea, Taiwan, Singapore, and Hong Kong; (5) the ASEAN (Association of South East Asian Nations) countries of Malaysia, Thailand, Indonesia, and the Philippines; and (6) Oceania, comprising the smaller Pacific islands, Australia, and New Zealand.

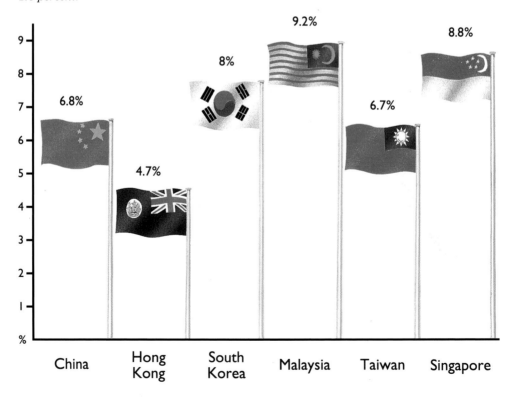

The press used the phrase "young tigers" for the countries of East Asia that expanded most rapidly. The term was not carefully defined. Judged by annual growth rate of GDP, Thailand, with a 1988 rate of 11 percent compared with Japan's 5.7 percent, deserves to be included in a list of "young tigers." But Thailand's GDP per head of population was some twenty times less than Japan's. For the purposes of this survey, therefore, we have limited our attention to the five smaller Asian countries with the highest GDP per head in 1990 — Singapore ($15,880), Hong Kong ($15,600), Taiwan ($12,670), South Korea ($6,730), and Malaysia ($6,140). Of the other two major Asian economic powers, Japan has already been covered, and China is given a chapter to itself. China is included not because its output is exceptional, but because its size, population, and phenomenal growth rate (11.2 percent in 1988) give it the potential to dominate the world's economy by the middle of the twenty-first century.

COMMON CAUSES

Economics is an inexact science. The circumstances leading to economic growth are not fully understood, nor are they ever precisely the same for any two countries. Nevertheless, the economies of the "young tiger" nations demonstrate a number of common factors that

Office workers in a Singapore street. The country's unusually high levels of savings, a contributory factor in its growth, is partly due to the falling birthrate as more and more women join the workforce.

Chun Doo Hwan, the army officer who seized control of South Korea in 1979 and remained in power until forced to resign by popular protest in 1988. The country's spectacular economic development continued to grow under his rule.

Every successful country (Taiwan, South Korea, Singapore, Hong Kong, Japan) has relied primarily on private enterprise and free markets to achieve economic development. Every country in trouble has relied primarily on government to guide and direct its economic development.

Milton Friedman cited in J. Sachs, "External Debt and Macroeconomic Performance in Latin America." Brooking Papers in Economic Activity, 1985.

helped promote their rocketing development. Some of these we have already met, as they also featured strongly in Japan's postwar development.

One important factor was the high level of investment in industry, labor, and infrastructure. Industrial capital came both from within the countries themselves and from without, particularly from Japan, the United States, and institutions such as the World Bank. This was different from the Japanese economic boom, the later stages of which were funded largely by domestic capital.

Like Japan, however, in the NICs domestic capital was a product of a high level of saving. By the mid-1990s East Asia, excluding Japan, was saving 36 percent of GDP. (The level of savings in Singapore, for example, was particularly high, at 46 percent of GNP in 1990.) Three reasons for this were the discouragement of consumer credit, the falling birthrate, and a longer expectation of life. These produced more people in the wage-earning/consuming sector of society who had fewer costly family commitments.

Investment in labor involved huge expenditure on primary and secondary education. As in Japan, higher education was seen as largely an individual responsibility. Good basic education created a skilled workforce and helped the broader distribution of wealth. The education of girls to the same level as boys tended to reduce the birthrate, but it did not lead to a rapid increase in the number of women in the top positions in industry and commerce.

Industry's first need was political stability. This often meant rejecting Japanese/Western style democracy in favor of more practical, authoritarian government. Until the late 1980s, for example, South Korea, was ruled by an unelected but economically highly successful regime.

Economic policy tended to follow the same practical path. As with Japan, there is considerable disagreement among economists about the role of government in promoting economic growth in the Asian NICs. Few governments adopted a completely hands-off approach. They preferred keeping a general eye on economic development, and intervening where appropriate over issues such as exchange rates, protectionism, and investment. This style has been termed "managerial capitalism."

Governments were not slaves to economic theory. They first decided what their economic targets were, then set about trying to achieve them by whatever means seemed appropriate. Their priorities were competitive exchange rates for their currencies, and low levels of government borrowing and debt (unlike Japan). There was government help for key industries, too. This took the form of loans, export promotion, and protection from imports. All the NICs spent heavily on the sort of infrastructure that assisted commerce — roads, railroads, and communications technology.

Some observers claim that there is another ingredient to the success of the NICs — Chinese culture. This is based on Confucianism, the system of beliefs attributed to the Chinese philosopher Confucius. It emphasizes obedience and hard work, qualities which were claimed to have assisted economic development. Whatever the influence of Confucianism, however, it does not explain why the NICs expanded when they did.

A supposed portrait of the Chinese philosopher Confucius, 551–479 B.C. After his death his sayings were collected and developed into the religious system known as Confucianism. The value placed on hard work and obedience in Far Eastern countries is often attributed to Confucianism.

SINGAPORE AND HONG KONG

CITY ECONOMIES

The similarities between Hong Kong and Singapore were quite striking. Both states were tiny (about 400 square miles) and densely populated (Hong Kong had a population of 5.8 million and Singapore 2.7 million in 1989). They had long traditions of being major trading centers with fine natural harbors. Agriculture had always played little part in their economies, and in both its share of GNP fell from 4 percent in 1960 to 0.4 percent in 1989.

Hong Kong remained under British colonial administration, while Singapore became self-governing in 1959. Nevertheless, their styles of authoritarian government were much the same, Singapore's People's Action Party being all-powerful since independence. Neither state is particularly interested in politics. Both have low crime rates and a strong work ethic, consciously modeled on that of Japan. Economically, the principal difference between Hong Kong and Singapore

Singapore harbor in the early twentieth century, when the island was a prosperous British colony.

is that the former relies on tourism, finance, and service industries to a greater extent than the latter.

SINGAPORE

Singapore became a British colony in 1858. Like Hong Kong, it was a flourishing trading center throughout the colonial period, with most of the wealth finding its way into European hands. The island became self-governing in 1959 and joined the newly established Federation of Malaysia four years later. In 1965 Singapore left Malaysia to become an independent state. Since then it has prospered as few believed possible. By 1994 its citizens were the second wealthiest in Asia. How was this achieved?

The foundations of Singapore's prosperity lay in history and geography. Long before independence it had a well-established reputation as a commercial center, based on traditions of free trade, expertise, and hard work. Secondly, the country's excellent natural harbor and strategic position on one of the world's major trading routes enabled it to take full advantage of the post-World War II expansion of the world economy.

Singapore harbor today, one of the East's great trading centers.

Lee Kuan Yew, prime minister of Singapore. Educated in England, Lee Kuan Yew returned to Singapore in 1951 and soon entered politics. He became prime minister in 1959 and guided his country into the 1990s and an era of unprecedented prosperity.

. . . we should not substitute the state for the parents or the family. If you bring a child into the world in the West, the state caters for him. That's dangerous. If you bring a child into Asia, that's your personal responsibility.

Lee Kuan Yew (prime minister of Singapore 1959–90), cited in The Economist,

But these advantages would have counted for nothing had the Singapore government, presided over by the authoritarian Lee Kuan Yew, not adopted policies that enabled them to be used to advantage. In 1985 the state was the largest employer in the country. It gave generous incentives to assist industrial development and encouraged the import of foreign technology, ideas, and money. Huge sums were spent on infrastructure to help business, particularly in the field of communications. In 1994 Singapore was set to become the first country in the world with fiber optics connected to every household.

The government also used its authority to maintain Singapore as a racially harmonious (discrimination against the Chinese was the reason why it broke with Malaysia in 1965) and relatively crime-free society. Singapore's refusal to follow the West's liberal attitude to crimes such as drug smuggling and vandalism attracted much attention in the Western media. The new prosperity built up a large, stable middle class, which on the whole was prepared to support the authoritarian government as long as it continued to preside over a growing economy.

The consequence of government supervision was the creation of a highly prosperous state, with extremely low levels of poverty and inflation, high levels of employment and adult literacy, fine medical services, and a life expectancy above that of Britain. In 1989 the economic base was well balanced between services (53 percent) and industry (36.6 percent), and there was every likelihood that the boom would continue unabated.

HONG KONG

China formally ceded Hong Kong to Britain in 1842. The Kowloon Peninsula was added in 1860 and the New Territories leased for ninety-nine years from 1898. During the first half of the twentieth century the colony flourished as a European and Chinese trading center. But it was a place where wealth could be made (largely by Europeans) rather than a place where wealth was widely distributed. The colony fell to the Japanese on December 25, 1941.

After World War II Hong Kong's economy received a lucky double boost. The first followed the fall of China to the Communists, when many Chinese business people took refuge in Hong Kong, bringing their capital and expertise with them. The second was the Korean War. By placing an embargo on trade with China, the United Nations gave unwitting assistance to the development of industry and commerce in Hong Kong. By 1962 *The Economist* magazine was describing the colony as "a show window of capitalism in the East."

Hong Kong might have been capitalist at the beginning of the 1960s, but it was also plagued with poverty. This soon changed. An annual GDP growth that sometimes reached 10 percent (the fourth highest growth rate in the world between 1960 and 1985) spread the new prosperity through most of society. By 1974 a mere 3 percent of the population lived in poverty. Exports rose from 70 percent of GDP in 1960 to 92 percent in 1987. Tourism flourished. The textile industry was modernized and moved into

Rich and zany — the concrete ship Whampoa, *set amidst a sea of new high-rise housing, is a shopping center that symbolizes Hong Kong's prosperity.*

synthetic fibers. By the 1970s Hong Kong was the world's biggest exporter of toys. By the next decade it had become an important center for the manufacture of high-tech electrical goods and the home of one of the world's most important stock markets.

Over thirty years the population increased from two million to almost six million, while incomes rose at over 6 percent a year. The colonial government was restructured to give greater power to elected representatives of the people. Primary and secondary education were made free and compulsory, and massive subsidies, or grants particularly for housing, lifted standards of living to among the highest in East Asia.

However, over the future of Hong Kong there hangs a large question mark. In 1997 Britain is due to hand the colony back to China. The Chinese have undertaken not to alter Hong Kong's economic or social structure for fifty years, but they have given no such promise regarding any further progress toward democracy. On the other hand, China needs Hong Kong. Guangdong, the Chinese province adjacent to Hong Kong, benefited hugely from the influx of Hong Kong-based enterprises and money. It is most unlikely that a country which is so successfully launching its own economic boom will want to interfere too strongly with a territory that in many ways was its model and benefactor.

The ultra-modern Hong Kong stock exchange, one of the most important commercial markets in the world.

SOUTH KOREA, TAIWAN, AND MALAYSIA

INTRODUCTION

The "young tiger" states of South Korea, Taiwan, and Malaysia are remarkable for their dissimilarities. Taiwan is an island, the major areas of Malaysia are divided by wide stretches of sea, and South Korea is a single peninsula. The culture in Taiwan is essentially Chinese. Malaysia is a combination of Malay, Chinese, and Indian, while South Korea has its own cultural traditions, influenced by long association with both China and Japan. Malaysia was part of the British colonial empire, South Korea and Taiwan had long periods under Japanese rule. Nevertheless, despite their different backgrounds and traditions, all three countries have played a major part in the late-twentieth century phenomenon of East Asia's economic expansion.

SOUTH KOREA

The development of Korea was even more spectacular than that of Hong Kong and Singapore. In fact, by outpacing postwar Japan and Germany, South Korea's growth was probably without equal anywhere in the world. Base statistics tell an amazing story.

● In 1960 South Korea's GNP per head was $82, the equivalent of Japan's in 1868. The level of industrialization was equivalent to England's in about 1700.

● By 1991 South Korea's population had almost doubled to 43 million. The GNP per head had soared to $6,500 and the overall size of the economy had increased more than 140-fold. It is estimated to double again by 1996. South Korea was the second biggest shipbuilding nation in the world by 1991, and the Hyundai Company the world's largest shipbuilding

American troops mine sweeping a mountain trail during the Korean War (1950–53). Substantial funds from the United Nations and the United States helped establish many new manufacturing industries in South Korea after the war.

The year 1992 marks the beginning of [South] Korea's Seventh Five-Year Plan under which the growth rate of GNP is projected to be 7.5 percent per annum . . . . At this rate of growth, Korea's GNP . . . will be $493 billion in 1996, making it probably by then one of the fifteen largest economies in the world.

From Asian Development Outlook *1992, Hong Kong, 1992.*

company. It also had the world's fourth largest textile industry, and ninth largest car industry.

It is not easy to see why South Korea should have developed any faster than the other NICs. The country had been torn by civil war (1950–53), then flooded with millions of refugees. Despite massive aid from the United Nations and the United States, the country was beset by unemployment, nondevelopment, and inflation.

The country's recovery began with an army coup, led by General Park Chung Hee, who became president in 1963. There is little doubt that the policies of the Park government — protecting domestic industries from imports, directing the economy, high spending on infrastructure — were major factors in South Korea's success. Also important were the legacy of education and business practice left by thirty-five years of Japanese occupation (1910–45), and massive assistance from the United States. This took the form of aid, purchase of Korean goods, and provision of technology.

South Korea's new prosperity had striking social consequences. Poverty fell from 40.9 percent of the population in 1965 to 7.7 percent in 1982. In 1988 Seoul, South Korea's capital city, was regarded as sufficiently well-run and stable to host the Olympic Games. By the 1990s the French fashion magazine *Elle* was available on the streets, translated into Korean, and American Haagen-Dazs ice cream was sold in the stores. In a single generation South Korea had become one of the most prosperous and sophisticated countries in the world.

The political consequences of South Korea's development were equally dramatic, leading to the downfall of

The gigantic Hyundai shipyard in Pusan, South Korea, 1987. By 1991 the Hyundai Company had become the world's largest shipbuilder.

the repressive regimes of Park and his successor, General Chun Doo Hwan. A highly-educated and well-off people, increasingly in touch with Western values and liberties, they were no longer prepared to tolerate an old-style authoritarian government. Student unrest at the end of the 1980s first forced Chun into reform, and then into granting a new, Western-style constitution with government by the people's elected representatives.

TAIWAN

The recent history of Taiwan is similar in some aspects to that of South Korea. Both had been Japanese colonies, both were governed by autocratic, pro-American regimes, and both lived under the threat of invasion by their Communist neighbors.

After World War II the Americans returned the island of Taiwan to the Chinese Nationalist leader, Chiang Kai-shek. When the Communists drove him from the mainland in 1949, he set himself up in Taiwan, calling his island the Republic of China. Until

Dogmatic and blind confrontation between politicians, between political parties, is a waste of the nation's resources.

South Korea's President Chun Doo Hwan in 1983, cited in Jack Watson, World History Since 1945, *1989.*

1971 the United Nations recognized Chiang's republic as the true China. As allies of the United States, Chiang and his successors enjoyed considerable financial and technological assistance, which they used to turn Taiwan into one of the most prosperous states in the region.

One of the biggest changes seen on the island was that from agriculture to industry. Whereas in 1950 agricultural produce accounted for more than 90 percent of Taiwan's exports, by 1990 the figure was no more than 6 percent. Over the same period incomes quintupled, poverty was all but eliminated, life expectancy rose to over seventy-three years and adult literacy rose to one of the highest figures of any NIC. A vast range of Taiwanese manufactured goods — from ships to semiconductors — were exported all over the world.

After 1987 Taiwan became a massive investor in other East Asian economies. By 1994 these investments had reached $12 billion. Of this, $1.3 billion had gone to the neighboring Chinese province of Fujian, and in the ten years following 1985 trade between China and Taiwan increased at an annual rate of about 32 percent. Some economists believe that before long China, Taiwan, and Hong Kong will form a single, gigantic economic bloc.

Not all the consequences of Taiwan's extraordinary growth were welcomed by the nation's traditional rulers. The liberalization of trade in the 1980s led to the rapid spread of fast food outlets, cosmetics, and other trappings of Western culture which tended to

A National Day parade in Taipei, the capital of Taiwan, 1974. At the insistence of President-for-Life Chiang Kai-shek (whose portrait heads the procession), Taiwan called itself the Republic of China.

Taipei, Taiwan, in 1989. Coca Cola signs and traffic jams indicate both prosperity and American influence.

undermine the traditional way of life. Industrialization brought pollution and urban overcrowding. There was also some growth in corruption and black market economics. In the 1980s the dominance of the Nationalist Party was increasingly challenged by the Democratic Progressive Party, demanding greater political freedom. Tension between the native Taiwanese and the Chinese community grew.

MALAYSIA

The areas that now compose the state of Malaysia — the Malay Peninsula, Sabah, and Sarawak — were former British colonies brutally occupied by the Japanese during World War II. Before their defeat, the Japanese encouraged anti-Western, anti-colonial sentiment in the region. Although this made continued British rule extremely difficult, practical problems made the British reluctant to grant full independence immediately after the war. Difficulties included racial tension between Chinese and Malays, political hostility between Communists and noncommunists, territorial disputes over which country should take possession of Sabah, Singapore, and Sarawak, and religious conflict between the Muslims and those of other faiths.

In the end, though, after the failure of the British Union of Malaya and Federation of Malaya, the modern Malaysia came into being on September 16, 1963. Once the country had come to terms with the secession of Singapore in 1965 and settled the long-standing dispute with Indonesia over the possession of Sarawak and Sabah, it settled down to a long period of growth and development.

In some ways Malaysia's new prosperity was the most surprising of all the "young tiger" nations. Although comparatively rich in natural resources — notably tin, rubber, and petroleum — these were beginning to run low by the 1980s. The government also had to cope with the traditional Chinese-Malay hostility, Communist infiltration and, more recently, the growth of militant Islam.

To control forces that threatened the unity of the state, the government kept a firm grip on both political and economic affairs. From 1970 onward it followed a policy of state capitalism, by which the government participated directly in commerce. Some businesses, such as the highly successful Heavy Industry Corporation of Malaysia, were entirely state-owned. This gave rise to the slogan "Malaysia Incorporated," suggesting that the whole country was a single business venture, backed and directed by the government.

Another government policy was to foster the growth of a prosperous and less politically-minded middle class, comprising both Chinese, the traditional business class, and Malays, the traditional ruling class. A third part of government policy involved attracting massive foreign investment. Between 1989 and 1991 $5.6 billion was invested in Malaysia, the bulk of it from Taiwan. The flourishing Proton automobile industry, which successfully penetrated Western car markets, was the result of close cooperation between Malaysians and the Mitsubishi Corporation of Japan.

Helped by these policies, the Malaysian economy grew at an annual average rate of about 7 percent from 1965. The year 1993 was the sixth consecutive one in which growth was over 7 percent, well above Japan and almost double that of the U.S. In 1990 Malaysia's GDP per head of population was $6,140, only just below that of South Korea and rising fast. Poverty had fallen to less than 2 percent of the population. Although the country's dependence on foreign trade and investment made it vulnerable to embargoes and withdrawal of capital, there was every indication that the growth would continue into the next century.

CHINA

EMPIRE, REVOLUTION, AND MAO

Three key requirements for economic development are a large population, providing a readily accessible market for manufactured goods, a plentiful supply of raw materials, and a stable government prepared to adopt policies that assist industry and commerce. The first two China has always had in abundance. The third did not emerge until the final two decades of the twentieth century. Before then the history of China was a long list of violent and tragic events.

The ancient Chinese empire, one of the world's oldest and most remarkable civilizations, finally collapsed in 1911. Government passed into the hands of the Guomindang (GMD) Party, dedicated to nationalism, democracy, and the people's well-being. But the GMD was unable to control the forces it had brought into being, and by 1916 the country had fallen into the hands of rival warlords. After years of civil war, leadership of the GMD (also known as the Nationalists) passed to Chiang Kai-shek. By this time a powerful Communist Party had

The old order in all its glory: the emperor of China arrives at his tent, where he is to receive the British ambassador in 1793.

Mao Zedong (1893–1976), founder of the People's Republic of China, was the son of a peasant farmer. Although the Great Leap Forward and the Cultural Revolution had been economic failures, he claimed to despise the later recognition of "American imperialism" while recognizing its necessity.

grown up, bitterly opposed to Chiang's Nationalists. However, in 1937 the GMD and the Communists agreed to act together against the Japanese.

Immediately after the surrender of Japan in 1945, the Communist-GMD civil war broke out again. Despite $6 billion of United States aid, by 1949 the GMD had been defeated and Chiang took refuge in Taiwan. Even though the authoritarian government exercised tight political control, China's economy went ahead by leaps and bounds for almost ten years after the Communist takeover. Following the enforced breakup of large estates and the transfer of land into the hands of small peasant farmers, agricultural production rose by some 4.5 percent a year. Between 1950 and 1959 the GNP climbed by more than 10 percent a year, with significant advances in manufacturing and heavy industry. Steel production rose from 158,000 tons to 5.4 million tons, and electricity generation from 4,310 kilowatt-hours (kWh) to 19,000 kWh. These figures were still pitifully low for a country of China's size and potential, but at least progress was being made. Suddenly, China's development came to a grinding halt.

In 1958 the Communist leader, Mao Zedong, called for a Great Leap Forward. This was to combine massive agricultural and industrial progress with a

reeducation of the Chinese people in Communist ways. Mao required the Great Leap Forward as a way of regaining control over the country, which he felt was slipping into noncommunist, capitalist habits. From a short-term, political point of view, the campaign was a success. In economic terms, it was a disaster. Farmers were forced into huge, unproductive communes, and grain output fell from 295 million tons in 1959 to 143.5 million tons in 1960. Coal and steel production declined by almost 50 percent. The value of Chinese exports was reduced by approximately $500 million. Even Mao admitted that it had been a "great catastrophe."

Deng Xiaoping, the last of the original Chinese Communist leaders. Born in 1904, he studied in Paris and Moscow and was among the heads of the Chinese Communist Party by 1955. Out of favor during the Cultural Revolution, by 1978 he had become the most influential figure in China.

In 1966 Mao again felt his hold on power waning. This time he launched a Cultural Revolution, typified by the slogan "Smash the old and bring in the new!" Gangs of young Red Guards rampaged around the country quoting from *The Collected Thoughts of Chairman Mao*, a hodgepodge of catchy but largely irrelevant quotations. Books were burned, scholars and experts scorned, and once more the economy dipped disastrously. During the height of the Cultural Revolution (1966–69) the output of grain, coal, steel, and fertilizer all fell. Overall industrial production declined by 30 percent.

The Cultural Revolution was not officially called off until after Mao's death in 1976. But by then the influence of the old leader was on the wane and that of his long-term rival, Deng Xiaoping, was on the increase. Under Deng's cautious leadership China finally began to realize its potential as one of the most powerful economies in the world.

THE CHINESE WAY

Deng's policy was to mix Chinese communism with the aspects of Western capitalism that best suited China's needs. His program had five main aspects.

The first was to stimulate China's economic development. One way that this was done was by allowing limited private enterprise, particularly in agriculture. The communes were broken up and individuals permitted to sell surplus production on the open market. Foreign capital was welcomed and foreign firms encouraged to go into partnership with Chinese businesses. Two of China's first commercial treaties were with Japan (1978) and the United States (1979). In 1980 the government designated Special Economic Zones (SEZs). Here what it called "market socialism" was to be free to flourish, backed by Chinese and foreign capital. New emphasis was placed on efficiency, enterprise, and market forces.

Hand in hand with economic liberalization went a degree of political relaxation. Mao Zedong, the great revolutionary, was no longer hailed as a god, but as "70 percent good and 30 percent bad." A new constitution was introduced in 1982. Efforts were made to improve the legal system to make it less of a political weapon. The Communist Party was distanced from government and the determination of economic policy. A degree of free speech was accepted and attempts were made to turn talk of human rights into reality.

Unfortunately, the reformers went further than the government was prepared to follow. After a prolonged crisis, the clash between Communists and democrats came to a head in 1989, when a pro-democracy rally in Beijing's Tiananmen Square was forcibly broken up by troops and tanks. In front of the world's media, many were killed and injured. Hundreds of reformers were imprisoned and the reform movement suppressed.

The third part of Deng's policy was to cut China's birthrate. As the population of China was estimated to rise to 2 billion by 2035 and 3 billion by 2075, undermining all chance of economic advance, the government introduced a One-Child Policy in 1980. It brought in a wide range of punishments and incentives to persuade couples to have only one child. Contraceptives and abortion were made freely available. Men and women were not permitted to marry before the age of twenty-four, and only after they had passed an exam in family planning. Even then they had to get permission from their Family Planning Officer to have their one child!

Mothers who gave birth to only one child received a bonus on their wages, free medical care, and extra food. However the policy was only partly successful. It was opposed because it was seen as an unacceptable restriction on personal freedom and also because it led to the killing of many female babies by traditionally-minded couples who wished for their one child to be a son.

China must with energy follow the Four Modernizations of farming, industry, defense and science. This does not mean shutting the door on the world or blindly opposing all that is foreign.

Deng Xiaoping, cited in Peking Review, *1978.*

A student of astronomy in the Observatory of Kunming. China is eager to develop high-tech industry as well as produce mass-market goods.

The fourth aspect of Deng's policy was the modernization of China's armed forces. However, with the ending of the Cold War in the early 1990s and with ever-increasing cooperation with the West, by the 1990s this drive had become less important than the other three. In 1990 the country was spending only 1.6 percent of GDP on the military (compared with 4.8 percent by Taiwan, for example) and the official figure had fallen by 1.7 percent since 1980. There are suggestions, however, that the defense budget considerably understated the true extent of military spending.

Finally, Deng called for China to catch up with the rest of the world in science, technology, and education. By attacking all things Western and encouraging students to despise their teachers, the Cultural Revolution had all but destroyed China's education system. A whole generation had grown up with little scientific knowledge and research projects had been starved of funds. The task facing the government was gigantic. Nevertheless, by 1987, 83 percent of all Chinese enjoyed some sort of basic education and the adult literacy rate had risen to 73 percent. The universities were flourishing once more. In 1990 twice as many engineers graduated in China as in the United States. Gradually China was beginning to develop the skills and technology necessary to compete in world markets.

THE GIANT AWAKES

The consequences of China's economic recovery are only just beginning to be felt in the wider world. They are, nevertheless, impressive.

By turning away from communal farming and allowing market forces into agricultural production, China increased grain production from 143.5 million tons in 1960 to 425 million tons in 1990. This meant that despite the population growth (estimated to have topped 1.3 billion in 1991), China needed to import considerably less food. This was reflected in import and export figures. In 1980 China's exports were worth $18 billion and its imports $20 billion. Ten years later the export figure had reached $72 billion and that for imports $64 billion.

The overall speedup in the growth of China's economy was staggering. In the decade 1960–70 it grew by 4 percent per year. By 1980–90 this had risen to 8.5 per-

A model for the development of Shanghai, the Chinese city that is rapidly becoming one of Asia's leading commercial centers.

cent per year, the highest figure of any major industrial country. The NICs' average was 8.3 percent, Japan's 4.4 percent, the United States' 2.8 percent and the world average 2.7 percent. But even this remarkable figure does not do justice to what was happening in the coastal SEZs, as this table shows :

PROVINCE	POPULATION	GROWTH OF ANNUAL GNP, 1980-91	NUMBER OF JAPANESE COMPANIES
Guangdong	64 million	13.9%	67
Fujian	30 million	12.7%	19
Shandong	86 million	10.8%	18
Liaoning	40 million	7.4%	46

Together Guangdong and Hong Kong (part of China from 1997) form the largest economy in Southeast Asia. In the 1980s Guangdong attracted some $20 billion in foreign investment, helping to make the total economy of southern China three times greater than that of any other economy in the region.

Economic development brought most Chinese a marked increase in wealth and living standards. The GDP per head rose from $85 in 1960 to $370 in 1991.

Young Chinese on the streets of Shanghai. Scenes like these would have been unimaginable in the time of Mao Zedong.

Over the same period life expectancy at birth rose from forty-three to sixty-nine years, and the mortality rate for under-fives fell from 203 to 43 per thousand. The average Chinese citizen was still a long way from sharing the sort of living standard enjoyed by those living in Japan or the NICs, but adequate housing, sanitation, public transportation, medical care, and education were coming to be seen as the norm rather than the exception.

China's achievement, however, must not be overestimated. In 1993 the economy was still only one tenth the size of Japan's. Moreover, there were those who believed China's development was doomed to failure. They cited two basic reasons for this. The first was the population problem. Despite the One-Child Policy, the population continued to grow at too fast a rate for the economy to keep pace for long. The second was China's precarious political position. The balance between political repression and economic liberalization was tricky to maintain. As the turmoil of the Mao era and the Tiananmen Square incident had shown, the country could descend into chaos once more. Prolonged or serious violence would lead to the prompt withdrawal of invaluable overseas investment. Were that to happen, the advances of the 1970s and 1980s would wither away even more swiftly than they had arisen.

Western economics, yes. Western politics, no. In June 1989 Chinese soldiers massacred over two thousand pro-democracy protesters in Beijing's Tiananmen Square. Here a citizen of Beijing stands in front of a convoy of tanks on the Avenue of Eternal Peace.

THE WORLD TURNS EAST

ECONOMIC CONSEQUENCES

The immediate consequences of the shift of world economic power to the Pacific Rim were clear by the mid-1990s. Along the Rim itself, millions had been lifted out of poverty and given the means to enjoy lifestyles previously only dreamed of or glimpsed in television movies. And the boom is expected to continue, so that by the year 2000 there will be some one billion Asian consumers — people with sufficient income to buy manufactured goods such as televisions, washing machines, and automobiles. But with the benefits of industrialization came new headaches. It is estimated that on still winter days the air quality in China's northern cities is up to twenty times poorer than the worst level acceptable in the West.

The economic effects of the Pacific Rim expansion on the older Western economies were threefold. Many were forced to withdraw from areas in which they could no longer compete, such as shipbuilding and the automobile industry. In their place they concentrated on areas of business in which they could hold their own, such as aerospace and insurance. This caused wide-

A sea change is underway in the world economy, as the center of world industry moves from the North Atlantic to the Pacific. The long-held economic wealth and power of the Western economies is now being increasingly shared by East Asia's hundreds of millions. The map of world business and industry is being redrawn as East Asia's economies continue their extraordinary rates of growth.

From James C. Abegglen, Sea Change: Pacific Asia as the New World Industrial Center, *1994.*

The Haishen Supermini, China's first attempt to produce a car cheap enough for ordinary Chinese families to afford.

spread economic dislocation and unemployment.

The second effect was to force the traditional economies to adopt Asian — particularly Japanese — methods of business. This meant breaking down the traditional worker-manager divide and building up a stronger corporate identity. Greater emphasis was placed on productivity, investment, and market research. Of course, none of this was new — particularly in the successful economies of the United States and Germany —but in some ways the Japanese had re-invented them. As, in the early part of the century, the Japanese had looked to the West for guidance, in the 1980s and 1990s the West was looking back to Japan.

A third consequence of the rise of the Pacific Rim as a major economic force was the banding together of several countries to form gigantic blocs with huge manufacturing and trading powers. They felt that to some extent this had been forced on them by what they believed were unfair restrictions on those trying to break into Asian markets. Whether the banding together of the North American countries and those of the European Union will help or hinder world trade remains to be seen. The successfully completed round of GATT talks in 1993 may herald a new era of more open world trade. On the other hand, it is possible that the three competing blocs — Europe, East Asia, and North America — will become more protectionist, thereby hindering their own development and condemning the Third World to continued poverty.

> It is now likelier than not that the most momentous public event in the lifetime of anybody reading this . . . will turn out to have been the modernization of Asia.
>
> The Economist, 1993.

POLITICAL CONSEQUENCES

The short term political consequences of the rise of the Pacific Rim were relatively straightforward. They involved demands by the United States that Japan and its prosperous neighbors play a greater role in preserving world peace. Japan's modest contribution to the United Nations force in the 1990–91 Gulf War, for example, drew considerable criticism from both the United States and Europe. Japan, on the other hand, was eager to do everything it could to present itself as a peace-loving, responsible nation.

The question of China's relationship with the rest of the world is more complex. As a huge but inward-looking and chronically backward country, China had presented little threat to other nations, apart from those on its immediate frontiers. But China as an eco-

nomic and military superpower, which it might become in the twenty-first century, is an altogether different prospect. Japanese and, to a lesser extent, American policy was to assist in China's economic development, believing that a prosperous China would be a peaceful one. They hoped political reform would follow on the heels of economic development, as happened in South Korea. As a consequence, condemnation of the Tiananmen Square incident of 1989 was comparatively muted. It was in no one's interest to drive China from the community of nations.

Two other aspects of the rise of the Pacific Rim need consideration. One is the growing division between the developed and underdeveloped nations in the region. In the 1990s this was apparent in the smoldering hostility between South Korea and the nuclear-armed North. The other is what happens when the economic boom begins to slow down, as inevitably it must. Many economists seriously doubt whether the world's resources are capable of supporting the population of East Asia in the sort of lifestyle currently enjoyed by only a fraction of the world's population.

Both situations could lead to unpleasant confrontations, trade war, and even armed conflict. Racial, political, and religious toleration survive easily enough when everyone is getting richer. But the real test of the Pacific Rim's achievement will come when its rise is no longer current news, but history.

Slum dwellings in the shantytown along the river bank in Ho Chi Minh City, Vietnam. The growing division between rich and poor countries in the Pacific Rim region could cause conflict in the future.

There is a big danger that the Pacific-centred golden age on which the world is launched could end in ... awful Asian wars a couple of decades hence.

The Economist, 1993.

GLOSSARY

ASEAN
Association of South East Asian Nations.

assets
All items of value, including money.

budget
Proposed expenditure.

capital
Money for investment.

Cold War
Bitter hostility which does not break out into fighting.

commune
An agricultural community in Communist countries, and more generally, a group of people living together.

communism
The political system based on an all-powerful state and the abolition of private property.

competitive exchange rates
The value of a unit of currency (money) in a specific country compared to the value of a similar unit in other nations.

conglomerate
A group of businesses under one management.

coup
Overthrow of a government.

diet
Governing assembly.

disposable income
Income that remains after taxes have been paid.

embargo
A ban on trade or a single product.

European Union
A confederation of European nations organized to bring about economic and political unity, formerly known as the European Community.

exports
Goods sold to one country by another.

foreign exchange controls
Legal controls imposed by a government on the ability of persons, businesses, or others to hold, receive, or transfer foreign currency.

GATT
General Agreement on Trade and Tariffs, an international agreement to promote world trade.

GDP
Gross domestic product, the total value of a country's home industry and commerce.

GMD
The Guomindang, or Chinese Nationalist Party.

GNP
Gross national product, the total value of all a country's industry, trading, and commerce, at home and overseas.

gold standard
Having a paper currency backed in full by gold.

hyperinflation
A massive fall in the value of money.

imports
Goods bought by a country from another.

Indochina
Southeastern peninsula of Asia.

inflation
A fall in the value of money.

infrastructure
The basic building needs of an industrial society, such as roads, railroads, and water supplies.

investment
Money put into an enterprise.

keiretsu
Japanese business conglomerates.

League of Nations
The international organization set up in 1919 to help bring about world peace and cooperation.

Left wing
A group inclined toward socialist or Communist beliefs.

Marxism
Communism advocated by the German philosopher Karl Marx.

monopoly
Complete control over a sector of industry.

NIC
Newly Industrializing Country.

Pacific Basin
The area of the Pacific Ocean and the countries within it and those which border it.

Pacific Rim
The countries within or bordering the western part of the Pacific Ocean.

protectionism
The practice of protecting a country's domestic manufactures by blocking imports.

repatriation
To be returned to one's home country.

SCAP
Supreme Commander of the Allied Powers in Japan.

stock exchange
A place where stocks and shares can be bought and sold.

United Nations
The international organization set up in 1945 to help bring about world peace, understanding, and cooperation.

wholesale price index
A means of determining changes in prices set by manufacturers and wholesalers for products before the goods reach the retail market.

World Bank
A United Nations organization established in 1945 to assist world economic development.

zaibatsu
Japanese family-owned business conglomerates.

TIMELINE

1842 — Hong Kong becomes a British colony.

1854 — United States forces Japan to open certain ports to Western traders.

1858 — Singapore becomes a British colony.

1868 — Meiji Restoration begins Westernization of Japan.

1871-73 — Japanese Iwakura Mission to West.

1877 — Bank of Japan founded.

1894 — Treaty ports system ended.

1894-95 — Sino-Japanese War.

1902 — Anglo-Japanese Alliance.

1904-05 — Russo-Japanese War.

1910 — Japan annexes Korea.

1911 — Chinese Revolution.

1914-18 — World War I.

1919 — Japan joins League of Nations.
— Japan National Essence Society founded.

1922 — Washington Naval Treaty between the United States, Britain, and Japan signed.

1929 — World economic depression begins.

1931 — Mukden incident leads to Japan seizing Manchuria.

1937 — Japan invades northern China.

1939-45 — World War II.

1940 — Japan floats idea of Greater East Asia Co-prosperity Sphere.

1941 — Japanese attack on Pearl Harbor leads to war in Far East.

1941-42 — Much of East Asia falls to Japan.

1945 — Japan surrenders to the United States.
— Allied forces occupy Japan.
— Korea divided between North and South.

1947 — New Japanese constitution comes into effect.

1948 — New Japanese five-year plan starts.

1949 — Chinese Nationalists set up in Taiwan.

1950-53 — Korean War.

1951 — Japan and United States sign formal peace treaty in San Francisco.

1952 — Allied occupation of Japan ends.

1954 — U.S.-Japan Mutual Security Treaty signed.

1955 — Japanese Democratic and Liberal Parties merge.

1956 — Japan admitted to United Nations.

1958 — China's Mao Zedong calls for a Great Leap Forward.

1959 — Singapore becomes self-governing.

1960 — Japanese opposition to renewal of Japan-U.S. Security Treaty expressed.

1961 — Japan begins buildup of its Defense Force.

1963 — Malaysia becomes an independent state.

1964 — Tokyo Olympics.

1965 — Japanese exports outvalue imports for the first time since the war.
— Singapore leaves Malaysia.

1965-73 — U.S. military involvement in Vietnam.

1966 — Mao Zedong announces China's Cultural Revolution.

1967 — Japanese Pollution Prevention Law passed.
— ASEAN formed.

1969 — Japanese student unrest is at its height.
   — Chinese-Malay race riots break out in Malaysia; parliamentary government suspended until 1971.

1971 — U.S. and China détente begins.
   — Communist China recognized by the UN.

1973 — World oil crisis occurs.
   — Japan eases import controls.

1976 — Death of Mao Zedong.

1978 — China-Japan Peace and Friendship Treaty formed.

1980 — China establishes Special Economic Zones.
   — China launches One-Child Policy.

1982 — New constitution in effect in China.

1987 — Widespread student unrest in South Korea leads to a liberalization of politics.

1988 — Seoul Olympics.
   — Japan sets out International Co-operation Initiative.

1989 — Chinese government suppresses pro-democracy movement in Tiananmen Square.

1993 — New round of GATT talks completed.

1997 — Hong Kong reverts to China.

FURTHER READING

Auakian, Monique. *The Meiji Restoration and the Rise of Modern Japan.* Silver Burdett, 1991

Baines, John. *Japan.* Raintree Steck-Vaughn, 1994

Black, Wallace B. and Blashfield, Jean F. *Island Hopping in the Pacific.* Macmillan, 1992

Carter, Alden R. *China Past – China Future.* Watts, 1994

Dolan, Sean. *Chiang Kai-Shek.* Chelsea House, 1989

Dubois, Jill. *South Korea.* Marshall Cavendish, 1993

Dudley, William, ed. *Japan: Opposing Viewpoints.* Greenhaven, 1989

Fyson, Nance L. *Hong Kong.* Raintree Steck-Vaughn, 1990

—— *Indonesia.* Raintree Steck-Vaughn, 1990

Hoobler, Dorothy and Hoobler, Thomas. *Chinese Portraits.* Raintree Steck-Vaughn, 1992

—— *Japanese Portraits.* Raintree Steck-Vaughn, 1994

—— *Showa: The Age of Hirohito.* Walker & Co., 1990

Langone, John. *In the Shogun's Shadow: Understanding a Changing Japan.* Little, Brown & Co., 1994

Layton, Lesley. *Singapore.* Marshall Cavendish, 1991

Major, John S. *The Land and People of Malaysia and Brunei.* HarperCollins, 1991

Marrin, Albert. *Mao Tse-Tung and His China.* Puffin Books, 1993

Phillips, Douglas A. and Levi, Steven C. *The Pacific Rim Region: Emerging Giant.* Enslow, 1988

Ross, Stewart. *China since Nineteen Forty-Five.* Watts, 1989

Snodgrass, Mary E. *Japan and the United States: Economic Competitors.* Millbrook, 1993

Steele, Phillip. *China.* Raintree Steck-Vaughn, 1990

Tames, Richard. *Japan Since Nineteen Forty-Five.* Trafalgar Square, 1989

Wee, Jerrie. *Taiwan.* Chelsea House, 1988

INDEX

ACKNOWLEDGMENTS

The publishers are grateful to the following for permission to reproduce photographs:

Cover photo (large): Tony Stone Images
Cover photo (small): Popperfoto
Hulton Deutsch Collection: pages 11, 49, 52, 58, 61;
Hutchison Library: page 37; Magnum: pages 6, 27,
31, 57, 59, 63, 65, 66, 67; Peter Newark's Historical
Pictures: page 62; Peter Newark's Military Pictures:
pages 18, 22; Popperfoto: pages 8, 12, 13, 20, 24, 25,
42, 48, 50, 53; Popperfoto/Reuter: pages 28, 68, 69;
Range/Bettmann: page 16; Range/Bettmann/UPI:
pages 21, 40, 56; Range/Reuter/Bettmann: pages 39,
43; Reuters/Bettman: page 45; Tony Stone Images:
pages 33, 35, 38, 47, 51, 54, 71.

Flags on page 46 by The Maltings Partnership.

© Evans Brothers Limited 1995